MW01223049

ALSO BY JAMES F. CIRRINCIONE

Taking Depositions

BUSINESS LAW
FROM WALL STREET TO YOUR STREET

James F. Cirrincione

JCOM
JCOM Publishing
Yonkers, New York

JCOM Publishing
Yonkers, New York
Copyright © 2020 by James F. Cirrincione
All rights reserved.

Names: Cirrincione, James F. author.
Title: Business Law / James F. Cirrincione
Description: First edition

ISBN 9798673893470

To Patricia Robert, who made this book possible.

TABLE OF CONTENTS

PREFACE

Your author has utilized many texts while teaching business law, over the years. Most of the books were incredibly heavy and incredibly expensive.

They also covered areas of the law I had rarely heard of. It seemed some of the texts were so extensive they could have served as the basis for business law 1, 2, 3, and 4!

And, yet, there were flaws. Most were very shallow in the litigation areas your narrator is familiar with. There were some outright mistakes with legal definitions. It was obvious that most of the authors were not practicing lawyers, in a gritty jurisdiction like New York City.

So, in the end, there was a desire to write a text myself. My students needed a volume with more depth in the areas where businesses frequently encounter the law. A more practical approach was also necessary for pupils who had sometimes just put in a 12 hour day working in a Bronx lab, or a showroom in Manhattan. This work is the result.

I apologize for the lack of brightly colored pictures and text boxes. I felt they weren't needed.

I ardently hope the reader will be will enlightened and entertained.

JFC
Yonkers, New York

INTRODUCTION

The first issue is, what is to be included in this volume? Some schools teach multiple courses in the area, so that can be a subject of debate.

This text is tailored to what the author lectured on, the basics of business law in America today. This volume is, therefore, a general, surface treatment of the subject. It cannot reach into the depths of modern law for deep debate. We will leave that to others.

The beginning of this text is a typical refresher on the U.S. legal system, because a foundation is needed about how our society regulates conduct, how laws are made, and where laws can be found, before getting into the elements of business torts and crimes.

WHY DO WE STUDY IT?

Just before we get into the meat of our studies, I would like to pause and explain what you, as a future manager, are facing.

You are facing trouble. Somewhere ahead in your wonderful career, whatever you have chosen it to be, is lurking what we in America call "a company legal problem." It may fester for months and you'll see it coming, or it may happen in two hours when your company's crooked accountant steals the company's entire quarterly earnings, and flees to Venezuela. It happens.

So, here is a list for you of the major legal danger areas for you and your firm. You will see, almost all the subjects we study will relate to these problems.

First, a disclaimer: This analysis is a culmination of experience and study. It is far from original.

YOUR CONTACT WITH "THE LAW"

The most common ways you will personally encounter law is getting a parking ticket or a summons. But, for businesses, law comes from many different directions, usually aimed at the company's bank account. First, consider the employees. History has proven they can be a rich source of litigation and legal problems.

Employees may be "whistle blowers," and expose a company to legal action. Or they may be injured on the job, or claim they were discriminated against, or that a hostile atmosphere was created in the workplace. Embezzlement and the evaporation of company funds, by a trusted worker, is always a threat.

Customers can be a source of litigation. A display stands falls over and hurts a patron, or they trip and fall, or they steal. Or customers are treated poorly, or slander the company.

Other companies and parties can cause legal issues with regard to leases, patents, competition, contracts and illegal conduct. Insurance companies have sometimes collected premiums in the past, and then refused to pay fair claims.

There are many other avenues of legal contact for a business, or employer. Regulatory issues, depending on the industry, are huge today. Some businesses must obey ancient, obscure laws, written on reams of paper no one ever reads nor updates anymore!

Add to the mix financing, stock issues, tax matters, searches and seizures, internal management, and you can see how businesses today face a possible quagmire of legal difficulties, if not carefully managed.

HELPING YOUR CASE AND YOUR LAWYERS

The main way managers and employees of businesses can legally help the enterprise they work for, is by keeping meticulous records, and maintaining a stable, skilled work force.

This was demonstrated again and again as your author tried jury cases in New York. Businesses that kept clear, honest records, and still had smart, faithful employees who could make sense of them, repeatedly got better litigation results than other firms. They were, at least, always able to mount a clear, rational position in court.

With clear evidence contained in a company's records, a judge or jury can follow a firm's decision making process. The company's litigation team can present the client in the best light, and show that the organization "comes to court with clean hands." This can be crucial in litigation where blame must be placed on one or more parties.

When your narrator represented companies with poor record keeping, the results often showed it. Their records were harder to get into evidence. When submitting business records in a courtroom, an honest chain of custody of who made the records, and how they were maintained, is critical. Because of high employee turnover, lack of training and employee apathy, we often could not prove that a company's written records were accurate. So they often could not be admitted into evidence. Even worse, in these situations, my adversaries were skillful enough (especially in big cases) to reveal my client's confusion, poor training and sloppiness during the trial, usually with a resulting verdict against us.

A WORD TO THE WISE

By necessity, this book is a surface treatment of the legal concepts contained within it. Every single topic in this volume has a wealth of further information available at your fingertips. The reader is earnestly encouraged to use this book as a launching pad for more intense, independent study. Your depth of knowledge and comprehension will vastly improve.

So, let's go ahead and start our study of this fascinating, complex and dominating aspect of modern American life.

1. A FRAMEWORK FOR JUSTICE

WHAT IS LAW?

Here's an encapsulated summary of different authors and philosophers on the subject. To be a "real" law, a rule, regulation or other order has to have three elements:

1. A rule, regulation or order of some kind, stating what conduct is banned or required.

2. The rule must be "passed," or "approved" by some recognized king, group, ruler or authority.

3. There must be a good chance of punishment or sanctions, for violating the rule.

One can view this in the microcosm of the classroom. A professor can turn to a student and say, "The law around here is that you only wear blue shoes or you will fail this course." That's probably not "the law" at a modern, metropolitan school. The school's administration won't back the teacher up on that. So that's not a valid law in a class. It's missing element number two, and that also eliminates element three.

But if a professor says "You will turn in three papers or you will fail this course," now one has something that is probably valid as one of the "laws" of that class. It establishes the rule: turning in papers. It is likely already approved by the school's administration because that is simply how schools operate. For a sanction, the student probably will get an F if they ignore it.

WHY DO WE NEED THIS STUFF?

We need to "categorize" human conduct to administer justice. We need to be able to say "This was a crime." Our society needs to distinguish a thief from a murderer, for many different reasons.

The law functions to maintain a safe environment and provide some level of safety from criminal acts on an everyday basis. If you want to start a business, hopefully, the law should provide a framework in which you can operate, with free and fair competition. The law provides us with some stability. If you are discriminated against, are injured or lose profits unfairly, or if someone breaches a contract with you, the law should provide some kind of remedy to help you be made whole again. The law itself provides the methods used to change laws and enact new ones. So one purpose of law is to change with the times, in an orderly manner.

WHERE IS LAW LOCATED?

Sources of legal information can be important in one's role as a business manager. The most common areas people find laws relevant to their work is in the state penal, health and welfare codes. America's states have produced a plethora of laws on every subject under the sun, from zoning and building codes to adulteration of products and consumer rules.

An owner or manager can usually negotiate a town's zoning rules, or hygiene laws. But a mistake of law for a builder, or construction company, could be so costly that professional legal help is usually advisable.

A rich source of law for business are the federal agencies, since they put out reams of their own "regulations." Some of these law producers have been so prolific (America's tax code, for instance) that they have spawned industries that print not only the regulations themselves, but additional series of volumes interpreting the regulations and reporting prior cases.

Certain sectors of the economy need access to specific laws, so many industries rely on the very well known OSHA safety regulations. New York has an extensive Industrial Code governing a wide range of business activities.

If you ever worked in human resources, you know that there are lots of laws relating to benefits, taxes and discrimination that a company needs to comply with. Almost all professions and large industries have magazines put out by their professional associations. These can be a rich source for legal issues and advice for those businesses.

There are specific legal journals, newspapers and periodicals, but they usually cater to the professional legal community. Certainly, as a business manager, it pays to be listening to general media and social trends that might affect your business.

WHY ONE LAW AND NOT ANOTHER?

With existing law, there is always controversy and disagreement. There are highly educated writers, and well informed critics, who produce a lot of written material on what laws are needed. They, in turn, try to influence prominent, powerful people. In this way they can get their ideas about crime, finance, capitalism or anything else, enacted, regardless of how extreme those ideas may seem to others.

Intensely discussing the why, and how of what laws should be made, and how human conduct should be viewed, and categorized, is the study of the philosophy of the law. When an author writes extensively about a particular approach to the law, they are said to favor a particular "school of thought" concerning the law.

Throughout history writers and commentators have made their ideas known and their efforts have been labeled, such as the "Natural Law School" or the "Historical School." These philosophies, the reader needs to understand, have a tremendous effect, over long periods, on what laws are made. If our leaders believe history should be the basis of law, we will have a conservative country with slow change. But if they think law should shape our everyday moral lives, it's a good bet the laws and punishments passed will be even stricter.

HOW AMERICA WORKS

One can look at the marvel of our modern society here in North America and see a finely balanced, clock-like regularity to our legal lives. Murderers usually get convicted, mostly guilty people go to jail, and, as Billy Joel sings, "only the good die young."

But, if one examines the system more closely, cracks and chaos appear. It's like looking closer at the rapids in a stream. You see the turbulence, and the sheer unpredictability in the system.

HOW THE U.S. STOLE ITS LEGAL SYSTEM

America revolted from England in 1776. But, we weren't stupid. We knew a good legal system when we saw it, especially when we saw we could steal it.

The English system of judges, juries, case law and written, "codified" law was never the target of the American patriots. The fact that Americans were being taxed without a representative back home in England seemed to be the real irritant. So, after the revolution, the new United States kept the English legal system that was already in place.

Don't get me wrong. We didn't keep the English. We took their land and stuff, and threw them out. But we kept their jury system. We kept their idea of relying on similar cases that had already been decided ("stare decisis"). And we kept their idea that some laws were important enough to write down and vote on.

HIGH SCHOOL CIVICS

At this point, we need a review of the basics, to be sure we are all on the same page.

There are three principal branches of the government, right? There is the executive, the legislative and the judicial branches.

These were established by the Constitution. America tried to govern itself with something called the "Articles of Confederation," first. It was written in 1777 and ratified in 1781. After a few years, it was obvious the Articles would not work. There were disagreements about money, about postage, and about whether each state had an obligation to defend the entire country. The central government was just too weak. So a new document was needed.

Our fledgling country held a whole new convention, and, after a lot of haggling, the U.S. Constitution was born. It was ratified in 1788. Even then, we had not yet gotten it exactly right. Like debugging some new software, the Constitution still needed a few more immediate tweaks, and the Bill of Rights (a/k/a the first 10 constitutional amendments) was added in 1791.

WHAT'S A CONSTITUTION? WHAT'S A STATUTE? AN ORDINANCE?

A constitution is a specific type of law. Constitutions explain how to run big things, like a country, or a state. So the United States Constitution is called the "supreme law of the land." That's because the Constitution is like a bad roommate. It is always right. Any law that conflicts with it, is illegal and invalid.

What's a treaty? A treaty is another kind of law. It is an agreement between the United States and another nation. Treaties become one of the supreme laws that take precedence over all other American laws. That's why treaties have to be entered very carefully.

Statutes are written laws that are voted on and then signed by a president or a governor. Often, statutes will be passed based on the state needs of current events. The systems in Washington D.C., and the states, are substantially similar, except for the names. Laws must be passed by a lower house, then a senate and then they need the president's or governor's signature and, that's it, they become law. If the president or governor vetoes the legislation, the veto can be overridden by the legislature.

An ordinance is a local law, passed by a town, or city, concerning parking or other local matters.

Note the names you are going to encounter next, because the name of each of the branches of government tells basically what they do.

THE "EXEC"

The executive branch executes the law. The head of this branch is the president, on the federal level, and the governor, in the states. Through her or him, the executive branch proposes laws and enforces them.

The chief executive, as the president is sometimes called, can issue executive proclamations and orders. The proclamations are statements of policy or are ceremonial. They are not laws. They are numbered sequentially since George Washington's first one, in 1789. On March 13, 2020, President Trump issued Proclamation 9994. It declared that the COVID-19 virus outbreak was a national emergency.

Presidential orders are a form of temporary law, suggested by the wording in the U.S. Constitution, but not spelled out. Therefore, exactly how far this power extends, and precisely why it can be invoked, is not well understood, and full of controversy.

Presidential orders have also been coming since 1789. Like proclamations, they are each given a number, in the order they are signed. Then they are published by the Federal Register, America's official website for federal information. President Trump issued over two dozen executive orders in 2020, as of this writing. On April 28, 2020, he signed Executive Order 13917 during the coronavirus pandemic. The order streamlined the entire meat and poultry industry in America. It allowed the Secretary of Agriculture to move national assets around to help food producers meet the needs of the country.

Similarly, Governor Andrew Cuomo, of New York, issued his Executive Order 202 on March 7, 2020. It declared a public health disaster emergency due to the coronavirus. On March 20 he issued Executive Order 202.8, called the New York State on PAUSE order. It ordered all "non-essential" businesses to close on March 22.

These orders were largely voluntarily obeyed by the population at large, and there were few legal challenges. Often, by the time a legal challenge wends its way through the courts, the emergency has already ended. The legal challenge will then be dismissed, as moot. Most such challenges are based on basic foundational rights, such as freedom of religion, speech or movement.

In May of 2020, some businesses that opened in violation of the Governor's order in New York City were given tickets, with a $1,000.00 fine. They were accused of violating New York City's Administrative Code 3-108, which states that emergency orders, like Governor Cuomo's, are to be obeyed. Roman and McShane. "From a Tan to $1,000 Burn." *N.Y. Daily News*, 29 May, 2020, p. 4.

THE LAW MAKERS

The legislative branch has the word fragment "legis" in it. That's Latin for "law," so that branch makes laws, through the House of Representatives and the U.S. Senate. The legislature also controls the money the government spends. There are 435 voting members in the House, and 100 senators.

THE JUDGES

The judicial branch gets its name from "judice" - the judge. This branch judges all civil and criminal cases that come before it. This branch of government also sometimes judges the other two branches, and the laws they make, and how those laws are enforced.

The federal courts, like the state courts, generally break down into three levels: the lowest is the District Court, a court of "general jurisdiction," meaning that most cases generally start there, and this is where most of the trials take place.

The next level is the U.S. Circuit Court of Appeals. This is an appellate court that only hears appeals and can correct errors made in a case at trial. It's called the Circuit Court because the judges used to ride from state to state, in a big circular route, on horseback or in carriages, to hear the various cases.

If you appeal your case above that, then your case goes to the U.S. Supreme Court. It's a panel of nine judges that basically represent the "elders" of the

United States, with the most experience and knowledge to judge the toughest cases.

THE U.S. SUPREME COURT

The Supreme Court is very unusual in that it accepts very few cases from the thousands of people who apply to it. You cannot have your case heard by the Supreme Court by simply serving a notice. You have to file a special document, called a "Petition for Certiorari," which costs thousands of dollars to properly prepare.

Litigating at this level is very expensive. Furthermore, the Court will usually only take a case if there is a conflict between the states on a legal issue, or if a case represents a pressing federal question that the country needs resolved right away.

Lastly, the federal government has created some other special courts that your company may need to take advantage of. The Court of Claims is established for cases against the United States. For instance, you may have a car accident with a post office truck. Who would you sue? Well, actually, the federal government owns the truck and the driver will usually be a federal postal employee. So, you actually have to sue the United States of America directly! Normally, a citizen can't do that. The federal government is "immune" to such direct suits by its citizens. So, the Court of Claims was established to specifically allow people to bring legitimate claims against "the feds," and its agencies.

There are other federal specialty courts. There is a Tax Court that only handles federal tax cases. There is a Customs Court for tariff, and importing, issues. These are courts of "special" jurisdiction. You cannot bring a simple negligence or contract case in such specialty courts. It will be dismissed for lack of subject matter jurisdiction. These particular courts, by federal law, do not have the power to decide run-of-the-mill accident or contract disputes.

CHECKS AND BALANCES

This is a well known concept in American law that states that each branch of government can act as a check on, or balance out, the other. The president can veto acts of the Congress. The Supreme Court can invalidate laws passed by Congress and signed by the president. But the legislature can create courts and modify their jurisdiction.

A WORD ABOUT THE BILL OF RIGHTS

It is ironic that the Bill of Rights should come up in business law. But, within the first 10 amendments to the constitution there are some legal doctrines that affect business directly.

In 1976, in a case called *Va. Pharmacy Bd. v. Va. Consumer Council*, 425 U.S. 748 (1976), it was established that American businesses have a limited right of free speech. The case allowed advertisers of drugs to mention their prices in public advertising for the first time. This is considered routine now, but at the time, it was a big deal.

PROHIBITED SPEECH

If the First Amendment grants a right of free speech, are there any limits on that, other than for commercial businesses? As it turns out, there are several instances where certain words are, literally, against the law. A well known example is causing a riot by panicking a crowd with dire, but untrue, warnings.

But did you know that using words that are probably going to provoke violence can also be illegal to say? That's right. If you're being arrested, orally threatening a police officer or yelling about the arresting officers's mother will probably get you some additional charges.

One of the most common examples of prohibited speech, seen repeatedly on the Internet, is advocating the violent overthrow of the government. It is illegal in America to call for the assassination or injury of someone in government. The numbers of people who have been tripped up by this in newspapers, emails, letters or by being casually overheard, are huge. Most are settled with a brief discussion with the Secret Service.

Since the turn of the century, our nation has been very sensitive to any kind of terrorist threat. A case involving Brooklyn rapper Israel Burns, who goes by the name "Ace Burns," is demonstrative of the legal problems social media can bring. He was arrested, in June of 2020, and accused of making terrorist threats. He allegedly posted Facebook live videos that threatened to burn New York's Diamond District, if the city's mayor did not speak to a crowd that had gathered at the Barclay Center, in Kings County. Goldberg, Noah. "Burn It Down." *N. Y. Daily News*, 9 June, 2020.

An untrue statement that defames someone is also illegal, although the person involved has to go through the trouble of suing to prove its illegality.

Speech that is obscene is also illegal. But, in order to be obscene, the work has to have absolutely no artistic nor literary merit, at all, in the community it was published. It is very hard to prove particular videos and literature are obscene these days, unless you are judging it in a most conservative community.

GOVERNMENT AGENCIES

The executive branch and the legislative branch often team up to create "government agencies," and those agencies make an awful lot of law nowadays. You've heard of them in the news: the FAA, the DOT, the FDA, FCC, EPA, etc. You can look up what those names stand for. There's a lot of them!

Today, these agencies are controversial. They have been empowered to create law, then enforce it, and then judge, and punish, anyone who breaks the law they wrote. Critics have said it is "unconstitutional" (illegal) for an agency to act as "judge, jury and executioner." Plus, there are too many of them, they ruin our economy, and they are too expensive. What do you think?

An example of an administrative agency in action was the 2019 Federal Communications Commission fine against the Jimmy Kimmel Show, and ABC-TV, for misuse of the Emergency Alert System. Kimmel used a real "Emergency Alert Tone" in a comedy skit about the president's new alert system. ABC eventually paid $395,000 in fines. Ganz, Jami. "Feds Fine Kimmel." *N.Y. Daily News*, 17 Aug., 2019, p. 12.

PREEMPTION

There are certain areas of the law, which relate mainly to national interests, where the federal government is said to be supreme. Federal law in these areas preempts all other laws. For instance, the federal government is supreme in matters of aviation because we don't want to have an airliner obey 50 different laws as it flies across the country. The FAA is the result, and any conflicting state, county or city law is not valid.

COMING DOWN FROM THE HEIGHTS

We will also be discussing other legal systems in this text, besides the federal one. These are the state and local legal systems that one encounters more often than any others.

The U.S. Constitution specifically states that powers that are not specifically delegated to the federal government are left to the states. This is known as the states' "police power," and enables them to enact their own laws for the population's health and welfare. Each state a person is in usually has more power over them than the federal government because of this police power. Most of the laws you obey every day, such as traffic laws and crime statutes, all flow from this power.

Each state has its own constitution, which explains how the state is to be governed. Many pattern their state constitution after the federal one, establishing an assembly and senate, with the governor as the head, very similar to the government in Washington D.C.

State constitutions also create state court systems. Again, very similar to the federal structure, most states have at least three levels for their cases. The first court is akin to the federal District Courts in each state. It's a court of "general jurisdiction," meaning, if there is no specialty court for a case, it is filed there.

In New York State, we have a court of general jurisdiction based in each county. So, in the Bronx we have the "Supreme Court, County of the Bronx," which is located right near Yankee Stadium. In White Plains, we have the same court, but it serves Westchester County.

A verdict in the New York State Supreme Court can be appealed to the Appellate Division, New York's first level of appeal. These appellate courts serve several counties at once, and, in theory, correct any errors made in a case while it was in the lower courts. If a case is lost in the Appellate Division, a litigant may then try to appeal to the highest court in New York, the Court of Appeals, in Albany.

WHERE THINGS GET COMPLICATED IN N.Y.

Like the federal system, New York also has many other small, special courts, For instance, large cities can have their own city courts, so Yonkers, Mt. Vernon and White Plains have their own courts for small cases. Counties, such as Nassau and Suffolk, are free to create their own county courts, below the New York Supreme Court. Towns are also permitted to create what are called "Justice Courts" for legal matters that take place within their borders.

Over two centuries, New York's court system has grown unnecessarily complex and bloated. A lawyer may have a choice of three or four different courts to file in, when litigating a small case. It appears that repeated efforts to simplify our system have been thwarted by local political leaders who give out judgeships as political rewards. These back room politicians have stopped all efforts at making our court system more efficient.

THE "PECKING ORDER" OF THE LAW

Sometimes, laws conflict. But not all laws are equal. Like almost everything in life, some laws are more important than others.

As an example, look at how conflicted marijuana laws are today. Many state laws permit possession of small amounts. Yet, those laws directly conflict with federal law that presently completely outlaws possessing pot.

The entire structure breaks down like this: constitutions and treaties with other countries represent the supreme law of our country. Next in line are federal statutes. Next are the rules of federal agencies, like the FAA and FCC. After that, state laws usually take precedence. Below them are city parking and traffic laws and town "ordinances" - the little laws and rules that govern the smallest details of our everyday lives.

TERMINOLOGY

We need to start defining some very basic terms. In the study of the law, as with any discipline, the proper use of the professional terminology demonstrates whether a student or practitioner knows the subject. So this is a crucial area of study.

We have two systems in every state, criminal and civil. Criminal cases are prosecuted by a district attorney or state attorney. Criminal cases result in dismissals, acquittals, and sentences of jail terms and/or fines.

Civil lawsuits are usually brought by a plaintiff who is a private company or person. Civil cases result in dismissals, settlements or verdicts and court orders and money judgments.

Criminal and civil cases actually proceed in a very similar manner, except that the prosecutor acts as the plaintiff, on behalf of the entire state, when a crime has been committed.

Both civil and criminal cases are opposed by the party called the defendant. In criminal proceedings, the verdict has to be unanimous, usually by 12 jurors. Two or three alternate jurors are selected in case anyone gets sick. The alternates are released just before the jury begins its "deliberations," as their discussions are called. The verdict is either "guilty" or "not guilty" in a criminal action. There is no verdict of "innocent." In a civil case, the jury can be made up of only six people, and a verdict can be less than unanimous, such as 5-1. If the jurors cannot agree on a verdict, they are what is called a "hung jury," and a "mistrial" will be declared. The case is then either abandoned, settled or retried, at a later date, depending on the circumstances.

The prosecutor cannot appeal a not guilty criminal verdict, because of the 5th Amendment (more about that, later), but the convicted defendant can appeal. In most circumstances, any losing party, in a civil lawsuit, can appeal the verdict.

The party who appeals is called the appellant. The person who responds to the appeal is called the respondent or the appellee. Appellate courts do not hold trials. They study the written record, and the evidence, to see if a legal error was made in the trial, or in the proceedings leading up to it. If an error was made, the appellate court can overturn the verdict, modify it, or send that case back to the trial court for additional proceedings.

THIS CHAPTER IN A NUTSHELL

Before we go on to the next chapter, let's briefly review what we should have absorbed by this point.

We are studying a system of rules that have binding force that come from a recognized authority. These rules should promote the general good, and they are flexible to an extent, so they can change over time. The particular laws and rules passed depend on how people think about history, morals and prior legal precedents.

Our U.S. system comes mostly from England. Law is made up of constitutions, statutes and cases. Cases that have already happened are called the "common law." Written laws are called statutes or ordinances. Many federal agencies also put out laws called "regulations."

We know the plaintiff is the one who brings a lawsuit and the defendant defends it. An appellant is the one who brings an appeal and the respondent, or appellee, responds to the appeal.

2. HOW DO WE RESOLVE DISPUTES?

Since people appeared on this planet, one of our major problems, for each society, has been how to settle disputes between people. This was important because, as in the Old West, when there was no law, people took the law into their own hands. An innocent accident, injuring one family, could result in a revenge murder, when there was no mechanism to provide some form of justice or fairness. To avoid violence, which interferes with collecting taxes, the state has always had an interest in providing a system for settling disputes.

A (VERY) LITTLE HISTORY ABOUT LAW

Hammurabi's Code was carved into stone around 1,790 B.C.E., in Babylonia. There were 282 separate laws. One of them was the famous quote, "An eye for an eye, a tooth for a tooth."

Then the Romans came along. They also carved laws in stone, then put the stone in the middle of town. They allowed vengeance to be a part of their law. If you won a lawsuit because your servant got hit by a cart, you might win a payment, but you might also be awarded the cart. You could burn it in the town square if you wanted, to "make a statement." They also came up with the idea of writing a last will and testament.

Now, when we arrive in medieval times, the first litigants were made to fight with batons to the death to see who won the lawsuit. It was called "Trial by Battle." Believe me, they were tough in those days. If you were severely wounded, but barely alive, you still lost the lawsuit. How could this happen? Well, western society, at that time, was extremely religious. They felt heaven would do justice and unquestionably award victory to the proper legal party. 4 William Blackstone, Commentaries *347-9. This was mainly popular in Europe and England, in the 1100's. Some people were able to hire a champion to fight for them.

People noticed, of course, that the biggest, richest guys were winning all the lawsuits, beating the heck out of everyone else. So, they needed another form of justice.

So they next tried "Trial by Ordeal," probably beginning with the Inquisition. When the question was legal guilt or innocence, the usual treatment was to be tied helplessly and then thrown into the water. If you floated, you were guilty as charged! If you sank, they tried to quickly save you. But, if you drowned, well, you went to your heavenly reward completely innocent of the charges against you. Unk. author, Witchery's Web, www.witchery.ca. This practice eventually died out, no pun intended, and the ordeal was eventually replaced by evidence and character witnesses.

THE FIRST JURIES

The modern concept of juries began with the Anglo-Saxons, in 1215, with the signing of the Magna Carta. Nobles and "freemen" of England were finally allowed "jury" trials. However, the "jury" at that time was made up of the parties' friends and relatives. The jury did not decide the facts of the case, as they do now. Instead, the jury testified as to the character of the parties. They were what we call "character witnesses," today.

Nowadays, character witnesses are not a big part of the system. People are allowed to testify to how truthful a party to a lawsuit is, but only in certain types of cases and even then, in limited circumstances. It's mainly the jury's role to determine how truthful the parties are.

LOCAL HISTORY

A little bit of the history of juries in America was written very near where this writer lived most of his life. St. Paul's Church, which is now on Columbus Avenue, Route 22, in Mt. Vernon, New York, was the site of an incident deeply cut into the American biography. In 1735, it was the site of voting for a new governor. This was decades before the American Revolution. A publisher, Peter Zenger, was arrested for printing articles critical of the Royal Governor, named, ironically enough, Bill Cosby. When he was tried in Foley Square, in Manhattan, the jury acquitted Zenger in 15 minutes. The whole fiasco established the free press in the United States.

The basic takeaway is that people have tried, for thousands of years, to resolve disputes. So, how do we do that, today, in America?

A FRAMEWORK WAS NEEDED: A SYSTEM TO SETTLE DISPUTES

As previously discussed, after the American Revolution, there was a need for some kind of system for addressing private and public wrongs, and for settling disputes. The United States adopted the English system of law. This next section explains the basics of the modern American legal system.

THE CONCEPT OF JURISDICTION

The first thing a society needs to do in order to establish a legal system, is to figure out who, and what, is subject to that legal system, and exactly who is beyond its reach. This, basically is the concept of "jurisdiction."

Jurisdiction has three definitions in this context, and they can apply to all three branches of government.

DOES THE COURT, ARBITRATOR OR LEGISLATURE HAVE JURISDICTION?

Jurisdiction is, first and foremost, the legal authority for a court, panel or executive officer to hear and decide a case, or to act in some way, or to hold hearings, to decide what laws are needed. This is why you will sometimes hear a lawyer say, "The court does not have jurisdiction in this case." No jurisdiction? No case! When this happens in the midst of a legal dispute, it's usually an easy win for one side, and a tough, quick loss for the other.

CAN THE COURT, OR PANEL, LEGALLY CONTROL WHAT IS IN DISPUTE?

Secondly, issues of jurisdiction can also relate to the court's or legislature's, or even the executive branch's actual "power" to reach out and direct, or control someone, or something. So, at times, in court, you might notice a judge (or an arbitrator or senator) make a "finding," or come to some conclusion about an aspect of a case. Then the judge will write or say something like: "Since I have jurisdiction over this matter, I find the plaintiff is owed money in this case, and that the defendant's funds are in the First National Bank, account number 54321. Therefore, I order the First National Bank to release all the money in account number 54321 to the plaintiff, within one week." Although this is a simplified version of such an order, it demonstrates that the judge, or other official, can take such drastic action because he or she has jurisdiction over that case, the bank, and those funds.

So, too, can an arbitrator, hearing officer, senator or member of congress also obtain jurisdiction over matters they decide.

IS THE DEFENDANT STILL IN THE JURISDICTION?

Lastly, legal practitioners will sometimes use the word jurisdiction as a substitute for the geographical boundaries of a city, county, state or country. On the TV news you may hear a sheriff say, "We believe the escapee has fled our jurisdiction." That means the prisoner made it across the state line.

HOW DOES A COURT, LEGISLATURE OR AGENCY GET JURISDICTION OVER SOMEONE?

We will discuss the court system here. But keep in mind, other government institutions, such as federal and state agencies, legislatures, subcommittees and a host of other governmental entities, can also need to obtain jurisdiction over people and things.

To obtain jurisdiction over someone or something, the government, or the party suing, must ensure, and be able to prove, that three things happened:

1. They drafted and/or filed legal papers with the court, suing the defendant.

2. They gave the defendant notice of the upcoming proceeding against them, and

3. They gave that person, or company, an opportunity to come to the specific court, or the body handling the case, to give their side of the story.

If it can be proven that a party gave someone proper information that they were being sued, and gave them a chance to go to a specific court and state their case, then that particular court will "have jurisdiction" (power) over that defendant. It follows that the court may then make enforceable rulings in the case concerned, and, eventually, confiscate the defendant's property, levy fines, or even throw people in jail, if necessary. And this is true, regardless of whether the sued parties choose to defend themselves in court, or not, once jurisdiction is obtained.

The power to decide all the issues in a legal disagreement actually flows from those two abstract concepts, which can be disagreed upon, and debated: The idea that a person (1) received a valid, properly written notice, and the idea that (2) the notice properly instructed them where and when to go to court, and how to file papers, and argue their side of the story.

Ultimately, after all the evidence is in, the court, or the jury and the court together, will make a verdict, or ruling in the case. In civil cases, that verdict will ultimately result in a dismissal, if the defendant wins, or a dollar amount of damages, if the plaintiff wins. In a criminal case, there will be a not guilty verdict or else a fine or jail sentence will be imposed. The police, the court clerk and court officers will all follow the court's directions to impound property, handcuff, arrest, incarcerate, or whatever, because they are valid orders from a court, with jurisdiction.

THE JUDGMENT

In non-criminal matters, the amount of the jury's verdict will be converted to a judgment for money. Such a judgment is a recognizable legal debt, in a well known form, that can be filed in the county clerk's office. Once there, it is a permanent record that can be accessed by credit reporting agencies, banks and others. In New York, a judgment against you, or your company, is valid for 10 years and earns interest. If it is not fully satisfied by payment, it can then be renewed by the winning party for another 10 years. Judgments themselves are confusing, odd documents. But they do list who owes what to who, from when. They can be found and researched online.

THE SATISFACTION

When a person, or a company, fully pays any judgment, it is crucial that they obtain a satisfaction of judgment, or "sat," for short, from the creditor that was paid. When the "sat" is filed with the clerk's office, it extinguishes the obligation under that judgment, and puts the legal matter completely behind the company, forever. If a satisfaction isn't obtained, the paid judgment can resurface, years later, looking like an outstanding lien. Getting things straightened out then will be much harder.

THE SPECIFIC DOCUMENTS THAT CREATE JURISDICTION

Now, let's briefly look at the two documents that generally create jurisdiction: the Summons and the Subpoena. These are the two main documents, once served on you, that will nowadays subject you, and/or your company, to the legal orders of the judicial system.

THE SUMMONS

This document "summons" you to come to court. You will be walking to your car after work, or having lunch with a friend. A stranger will come directly toward you and say, "Are you 'So and So'?" He or she will already know you are "So and So," from a photo they were given. So, they may not wait for your answer.

Suddenly, their hand will shoot out, holding a piece of paper. You guessed it: it's the summons! Sometimes it comes out from behind a bouquet of flowers, or a magazine. Now, it's too late to run.
They won't even wait for you to take it. They will press it against your arm, or your chest. Then they usually mutter something like, "You've been served!" and they let it go and walk away.

They don't care if the summons falls to the floor. They don't care if you ignore it. They will have already studied your appearance, so they can fill out the form on the back of the document. There, they will swear they served you, and state the place, date and time when it happened. The form affidavit will also have your approximate age, height, race and gender. This is used later, if necessary, to identify you, if you try to deny that it ever happened.

If you do bother to read the summons, you will see how it conforms to the law stated above.

[EXAMPLE]

SUPREME COURT OF THE STATE OF NEW YORK
COUNTY OF WESTCHESTER
---X
JOHN DOE,

     Plaintiff,

  -against-   SUMMONS
                 Index No. 7777/21

FRANK ROE,

     Defendant
---X

To FRANK ROE
    10 Main St.
    Bronxville, NY

Greetings:

WE COMMAND YOU, that all business and excuses being laid aside, you appear and demand the complaint be served upon you, within 30 days.

Failure to answer this complaint will result in a default judgment against you.

Dated: Bronxville, New York
    March 9, 2020

             _____
             JAMES F. CIRRINCIONE
             Attorney for plaintiff
             1 Main Street
             Bronxville, New York 10708

First notice that the above form is clearly marked "Example." That's because it is illegal to create a fake or joke legal document. People still do, but it is against the law.

Next, note that, taken as a whole, the information in the summons supplies which court is involved, the name of the person suing, the time limit in which one must respond, and the opposing attorney's name and address. All those facts provide you with notice of the lawsuit, so the summons itself satisfies that branch of obtaining jurisdiction.

But the summons goes one step further, in that it tells you what to do: you must "appear" in the lawsuit, then demand the complaint, within 30 days.

Where do you demand and get the complaint from? From the plaintiff's attorney.

The document also satisfies the other concept of obtaining jurisdiction: the opportunity to be heard. Because you have the attorney's name and address, and the court involved, you have the means to answer the summons and make your defenses known.

The summons provided notice and the opportunity for you to be heard. Unless you can immediately show how jurisdiction is somehow lacking, or based on a mistake, the court now has jurisdiction (power) over you. Upon proper proof against you, it can now legally order you to pay money, do community service or to refrain from doing something that is bothering someone else.

THE SUBPOENA

The other way people and companies can be "hauled into court" is with a subpoena. It confers a different kind of jurisdiction. These usually result when someone witnesses an accident or a crime, or when someone has records that are relevant to a dispute that is being heard in court or in the legislature.

[EXAMPLE]

SUPREME COURT OF THE STATE OF NEW YORK
COUNTY OF WESTCHESTER
---X
JOHN DOE,
                  Plaintiff,
      -against-   SUBPOENA
DUCES TECUM

                                        Index No. 7777/21

FRANK ROE,

Defendant

--X

To   SALLY DOE
       10 Bronxville Avenue
       Bronxville, NY 10708

Greetings:

WE COMMAND YOU, that all business and excuses being laid aside, you appear and attend to the Subpoenaed Records Room, Ground Floor, Window 6, at the Supreme Court, Westchester County on the _____ day of _____, 2020, at 9:30 a.m. in the forenoon and at any recessed or adjourned date thereof, to give testimony on the part of the plaintiff, and that you bring with you and produce at the time and place aforesaid:

The certified, complete employment and medical records for JOHN DOE, DOB 6/9/90, SS# 001-62-7399, 300 Yonkers Avenue, Yonkers, NY 10704, from 2017 to 2020, including, but not limited to, performance reviews, attendance, health, payroll records, positions, titles, training, promotions, demotions and any accident and incident reports.

Failure to comply with this subpoena is punishable as a contempt of court and shall make you liable to the person on whose behalf this subpoena was issued for a monetary penalty and all damages sustained by your failure to comply.

Dated: Bronxville, New York
         March 9, 2020

                                      _____
                                      JAMES F. CIRRINCIONE
                                      Attorney for plaintiff
                                      1 Main Street
                                      Bronxville, New York 10708

The subpoena does basically the same thing as the summons, by providing similar information. All the same rules about serving a summons apply to serving a subpoena. But, instead of dragging the person into a lawsuit to get them to pay money they owe somehow, this document obtains control over someone, or some written records, so that they can be brought into court to produce evidence in the case.

TYPES OF JURISDICTION

Another thing business managers need to know about jurisdiction is that there are different kinds. The jurisdiction of a court, or legislative body, can be very broad and general, or very specific and narrow. Because of this, different types of jurisdiction have evolved for different purposes and objects.

"IN PERSONAM" JURISDICTION

'Don't be intimidated by the Latin name. This is the most common type of authority courts have over people. This is, simply, "personal" jurisdiction over a human being. When a person gets served with a summons, it confers in personam, or personal, jurisdiction, over them, onto the court. This is the kind of jurisdiction you need to sue someone, or force them to testify as a witness.

"IN REM" JURISDICTION

"Rem" means "thing," in Latin. So this is jurisdiction over things. Legally, we call all such objects "property." Property, in turn, breaks down into personal property (cars, jewelry, computers, TV's, radios, furniture and things like that) and real property (real estate, houses, condos and land).

Because disputes sometimes arise concerning these things, a court must have power over them to make rulings and decide who owns what. Usually, the objects in dispute have to be within the geographical area the court sits in. So, disputes about land in Westchester County must go to Westchester County Court.

The title to personal property is more varied, and with computers and a global economy, the rules are changing fast. Suffice it to say that, usually, the personal property or title to the disputed personal property, must be in the city, county or state in which the court seeking jurisdiction sits.

STANDING

Going hand-in-hand with jurisdiction is the concept of "standing." With regard to disputes, everyone in our society is allowed to have an opinion. But only certain parties are allowed to bring their actual claims for damages to court.

Simply stated, legal claims are personal in nature. They can be used to secure a loan, but they cannot be transferred to others who are not related to what happened. If you are injured, you can involve all sorts of people in your case, and promise each of them money if you win. But, it is still only you who can bring the case and you must prove it. You are the only one who has standing.

An example of a lack of standing is when you hear that a friend has had a serious car accident. Your friend can sue for their injuries. Your friend's spouse can sue for the loss of your friend's help around the house. You miss your friend. You feel hurt. You don't see them for a long period. But you cannot march into court and sue anyone involved. The law does not recognize a right to sue for friends' injuries. In this situation, you have no standing.

A REAL DISPUTE

Business litigation, concerning advertising, or business practices, must qualify as a serious dispute before the courts will entertain litigation concerning these issues. So, how serious does a legal wrong or injustice be in order to bring a lawsuit?

That answer comes from a well studied case in Business Law, *Harris v Time, Inc.*, 191 Cal. App. 3d 449 (1987).

This case concerned a three year old son of an attorney, Joshua Gnaizda. In 1985, the little boy received a piece of junk mail that stated he would be given a "versatile new calculator watch free for just opening the envelope." When the envelope was opened, however, the contents revealed that you had to actually purchase a magazine subscription to get the watch.

Joshua's father sued. As a matter of fact, he went even further and gathered others together, and brought what is known as a "class action," against Time, Inc. They claimed there was a breach of an implied agreement, unfair advertising and fraud. They demanded that Time stop making such mailings, provide free watches to recipients of the mailer and to pay $15 million in punitive damages to establish a consumer education and advocacy fund.

In a nasty decision, the California Court of Appeals said the case had to be dismissed because "The law disregards trifles." This case, the Court said, was trifling "in the extreme."

Therefore, cases involving junk mail and the misleading advertising of a free watch worth $20.00 do not rise to the level of a legal dispute that can be remedied by our legal system. A dispute over $20.00, in certain circumstances, may sometimes be entertained in a small claims court. But, normally, the entire state's legal machinery cannot get involved and such cases must be dismissed. The law does not provide people nor businesses with a remedy for every slight, mistake, or inconvenience they may suffer. Business managers must always evaluate if litigation is necessary, or advised, in the circumstances they face.

FRIVOLOUS LAWSUITS

New York, as well as many other states, has been wrestling with the burden of frivolous lawsuits for decades. The court system is stuck in a difficult position. The lifeblood of the court is litigation. Litigation is what often drives the law to improve. Law students are encouraged to consider bringing chancy, new lawsuits to help people obtain their rights and assist the poor and those who are not usually represented adequately in court.

But against this backdrop, the courts are swamped with cases that, to the objective observer, seem vengeful, or silly or without much real legal significance. So there is a constant balancing act that goes on, as the courts try to prevent silly legal actions but not put themselves out of business nor stifle new thinking and the discovery of new valid legal theories and claims.

In most states someone can be sued for malicious prosecution. That is, the bringing of trumped up, fake charges, or charges that are repeatedly filed and then dropped. This can be hard to prove and was not a favorite tort in our office.

In addition, New York has a specific court rule (PART 130, Rules of the Chief Administrative Judge) that allows a court to sanction any party, or lawyer, for bringing a frivolous lawsuit or for frivolous conduct during the lawsuit itself. This section, although typed by legal secretaries in pleadings all over the state, thousands of times a year, is very rarely enforced. The scandal of silly, stupid lawsuits, costing everyone time and money, and slightly increasing our taxes, and insurance costs, marches on.

A NOTE ON "CITATIONS"

The reader may have noticed some odd looking letters and numbers after the case name of *Harris v. Time*. That is the "case citation."

There are millions of cases reported each year. Systems are needed to allow legal personnel to quickly identify a case, and find reports about it in the legal literature.

In the aforementioned case, *Harris v Time*, the title of the case was followed by: "191 Cal. App. 3d 449 (1987)." The entire statement of the case name, with the information that follows it, makes up the citation, or "cite." It is written in a specific, useful form. Sometimes, there are slightly different forms of citations used by lawyers, but this is a good example of a basic one.

Because of the sheer volume of cases, the reports are bound into long series of separate books, each book in the series numbered from 1 onward. Both governments and private companies print such case law reports. In the example, the first number "191" means the 191st volume. The next part states which series the case is in. "Cal. App. 3d" means that book is in the third series of the California Appellate Reports, the official books put out by the state itself. This also indicates that the decision referred to is that of an appellate court, so it is a report on an appeal, not on a trial or a simple motion. The "499" refers to the page number the case is on, and the year of the decision is in parenthesis.

BUT WHAT HAPPENED TO JOSHUA?!

So, now we can understand why Time, Inc. is named in the citation. They were the party sued. But who is Harris? Well, as it turns out, the case was turned into a class action, before it was appealed. A class action is a lawsuit in which a small group of people act as plaintiffs, on behalf of a much larger group of people, who are also in the same legal position. So, somewhere along the way, Mark Harris joined the case as a plaintiff, thereby changing the caption, or name, of the case, forever.

VENUE

Lastly, before we leave these concepts, we need to discuss venue. The venue is the physical location of the court that will hear the case. Because the demographics from one local region to another can be vastly different, venue can be crucial to an entity's success or failure in a legal action.

There are a lot of reasons to change venue. Sometimes there has been a lot of publicity about a case in a local area. The court may agree to change the location of the trial on that basis. This was the case with the famous 1995 O.J. Simpson trial.

Other times the trial will be moved for the convenience of witnesses who have to testify. Sometimes the residency of a party or the location of the accident will decide the venue. Just be aware this can be a critical issue in any case you come in contact with throughout your career.

PLEADINGS

A case is begun by what are called "pleadings." Just as the name suggests, these plead each person's case to the neutral court.

The summons and complaint starts the lawsuit. The complaint contains a numbered list of each fact that the plaintiff, or the prosecutor, will prove to show that the defendant is responsible. In a civil, or non-criminal case, the issue will be: is the defendant responsible for the civil damages (injuries) done? In a criminal case, the verdict will be whether the defendant is criminally responsible for the crimes he or she is accused of.

In one's own small claims case, one can easily list the basic facts in a simple complaint. Other than in that setting, these documents are complex and always drafted by attorneys.

The "answer" is, appropriately enough, the answer to the complaint. It states exactly which facts are admitted and which are denied. It also includes any defenses the defendant claims. This is all done to simplify the resulting lawsuit. Assuming the documents are properly drafted, anyone comparing the written complaint and the written answer, side by side, should be able to clearly see what is in dispute and what isn't.

DISCOVERY

Once a lawsuit starts, the parties are actually forced by the court to work together somewhat. They must exchange basic written things like witness' names, accident reports, photos, medical records, and lists of claimed expenses and damages.

The parties can serve formal questions on their opponents, demanding written, sworn answers be given. Exactly which litigation tool to select is up to the individual lawyer assigned to the case.

Each side can depose the other in civil proceedings. The resulting deposition transcripts can be used to investigate the case, find more evidence, and impeach a witness in court, if they try to testify differently at the trial.

SETTLEMENTS

The overwhelming majority of criminal and civil cases end up being settled. This can be seen as controversial. In criminal cases, many defendants claim they ended up convicted because they did not have the means to combat a state of 18 million people who had unlimited resources to prosecute them. When a prosecutor offers to set a person free for "time served," if they agree to accept a conviction, few people have the nerve to refuse the offer, and stay in jail to eventually be publicly exonerated at trial.

In civil cases, insurance carriers representing defendants can wear down a plaintiff for years, dragging the case backward with needless motions and expensive, irrelevant discovery. When a final, small settlement is offered, just before trial, many people just take it and run, to put the whole awful experience behind them.

THE TRIAL

If the case can't be settled, it goes to trial. Trials are nothing like Americans see in the movies and on TV. The proceedings move at a snail's pace and dramatic moments are few and far between.

JURY SELECTION

Either side, in America, can demand a jury. If a jury is to be selected, that usually happens first. The jurors are selected in a proceeding called a "voire dire," which means to speak and hear. In New York, and many other states, the attorneys do the selecting by themselves. At other times, especially when the attorneys clash, a judge will oversee the selection of the jury. In federal court, the judge exerts more control over the selection of jurors.

Jury selection is supposed to be a probe to find fair jurors. Each attorney, in turn, gets to question the jurors and ask them if they know the parties, or their attorneys, and also how they feel about the case. However, behind the scenes, it is often a twisting, turning subtle wrestling match, with each side trying to prejudice the prospective jury in their client's favor, while appearing as innocent as the freshly driven snow.

What the lawyers are usually looking for is someone with average intelligence, who is calm, and not very opinionated, nor a leader. If disputes arise as to who should be on the jury or not, the court will make that ruling.

OPENING STATEMENTS / QUESTIONS / CLOSING STATEMENTS

Once a jury is selected, a court reporter will arrive in the courtroom to begin writing down everything said at the trial, in case there is an appeal. The court will then begin giving the jury some preliminary instructions. These will usually be extremely general instructions, explaining the basic claims, the order of the trial and, perhaps, what evidence is, who some of the witnesses will be, and the schedule for the trial.

If the judge has proper control of the courtroom, the attorneys in a jury trial are very limited in what they can do, in front of the jury. Many an attorney has been caught with a sloppy approach to the trial proceedings. Making statements while questioning a witness, telling stories, side remarks, funny looks, the rolling of eyes, grunts of agreement or disagreement by a lawyer, are all improper. All such events should be described "on the record" for the court reporter, and should also be objected to, immediately, with a request that the court order the attorney to stop it.

The lawyers in front of a jury may make one speech at the start: the opening. Then, they question witnesses. Then they get to make one last speech, at the end of the trial: the closing. That's it.

The opening statements in most trials should be brief. The plaintiff's opening gives a general account of what will be proven. The defendant's opening gives the outline of the defense to the lawsuit. Then witnesses are called.

In modern trials, with physician's and other experts' schedules, witnesses often testify wildly out of order. A jury may hear a defense expert testify before the plaintiff. But, traditionally, the plaintiff goes first, and puts in all of his or her evidence. Once the plaintiff's lawyer says "I rest my case," they are done. The defendant then puts in his or her entire case. When the defendant's attorney says "I rest my case," they are done. Neither party can put in any more new evidence, without the permission of the court.

Behind the scenes, out of the hearing of the jury, the parties often bombard the poor judge with motions, memorandums of law and other voluminous papers during the trial to influence the court to favor their side. There are often extensive proceedings and long arguments over the admissibility of evidence or the fairness of having certain experts give their opinion about the case.

After both sides finish, the plaintiff is sometimes allowed to go again, but only to dispute any new issues and evidence the defendant raised. Then the defendant may ask the court to put in additional evidence in rebuttal. This goes on and on, until both sides "rest," again, or until the court interferes, and forces both sides to rest.

THE CLOSING STATEMENT

The closing statement in trials, both jury and non-jury, are among the most dramatic monologues you will ever hear in the courthouse. Lawyers usually pull out all the stops and passionately try to persuade the court and jury of the validity of their position. Some of these speeches are so eloquent, they have been preserved and serve as fine examples of the trial attorneys' art.

CHARGING THE JURY

After all sides sum up in their closing arguments, the court then gives the jury the law. This is called charging the jury and, once begun, the courtroom doors are usually locked, often with a sign stating, "Judge Charging Jury."

Many people feel this is an odd way of doing things. The jury is told the law they must apply after all is said and done. That information would have been much more helpful had it been delivered earlier in the proceedings. Even the judging of the truthfulness of witnesses, would have been substantially aided had they known the laws they were going to use to decide the case at the time the person was testifying.

DELIBERATIONS

At this point in the proceedings, having heard all the evidence and all the instructions, the jury retires to deliberate, usually with a court officer just outside the door. The officer will respond if they need anything, or have a question for the court. The jury can ask to be given evidence exhibits and also to have testimony read back to them by the court reporter.

Deliberations have no time limit. The bigger the case, the more reluctant the judge will be to declare a "mistrial." If a verdict is not reached in a reasonable amount of time, the court will declare the jury "deadlocked" and order a new trial. If the case doesn't settle in the meantime, the parties come back and do it all again.

If a verdict is reached, it is formally reported by the foreperson, and taken down by the court reporter. If it's a criminal case, especially if controversial, a group of court officers will encircle the defendant, before the verdict is read. If it is "guilty," the defendant goes to jail immediately.

In the civil arena, the verdict will be reduced to a judgement, which the defendant will have to pay.

Any party can appeal the verdict because they lost or if they feel they did not win enough. A prosecutor, however, may not appeal an acquittal because of the protection against double jeopardy contained in the 5th Amendment. If there's an appeal, payments on a civil judgment can sometimes be postponed.

IN SUMMARY

This, then, is a review of the basic underpinnings of our American system of justice. There were, and still are, fundamental problems with this system. It is cumbersome. It takes years to get a decision. The appellate process is equally frustrating. It is a very costly system. The judges, the stenographers, the court officers, the infrastructure are all frightfully expensive. Then there are the costs of litigation: filing fees, investigations, deposition costs. Expert witnesses receive $10,000.00 for a few hours of testimony in an afternoon. And those experts can't continue testifying the next morning, because they are booked to testify in another case, halfway across the country, for another $10,000.00!

So, early on in our nation's history, it was recognized that a cheaper, more efficient means of administering justice was needed in America. That is the subject of the next chapter.

3. ALTERNATIVE DISPUTE RESOLUTION

In order to streamline the handling of disputes, and to make justice more available to everyone, different types of legal proceedings have been created to make handling claims more efficient.

Jurists and writers have tried to be careful not to "throw the baby out with the bath water." No one wants what is referred to as junk justice. So most of these attempts at making litigation more efficient are well intentioned and well thought out.

ARBITRATION

One of the most popular methods of resolving disputes in America today is by arbitration.

Arbitration can be thought of as the same type of proceeding as a trial: an in depth look at the evidence, resulting in a decision for, or against, one side. But the whole thing is usually conducted in a much more informal way.

HOW YOUR PARTICULAR ARBITRATION WILL GO

It is impossible to say, with complete certainty, how formal or informal any particular arbitration will be, because the parties are free to fashion this device into as broad, or narrow, a proceeding as they can agree upon.

Arbitrations can be agreed upon in almost any dispute. However, arbitration most often comes about by contract. The parties enter into a contract, and have already agreed that, if there is a dispute, it will be settled by arbitration.

The parties can have one arbitrator to sit as a judge, or hire three, or more, to act as a panel of judges. You can set limits on the time each party will have to speak and enter other agreements on what evidence will, and will not, be placed before the arbitrators.

It all depends on what each party can get the other to agree to and how the arbitrators run their proceedings. Some arbitrators are retired judges and they "run a tight ship." Their arbitrations can have formal opening and closing statements. They may allow motions before, or after, the arbitration hearing. However, another arbitrator may be a practicing attorney with special knowledge in your case's area of law. He or she may run the arbitration totally informally, having open, informal conversations about the case with no long speeches.

THE ARBITRATION CLAUSE HAS TO BE VALID

Almost nothing in the law is absolute and never changing. Although we can't go into depth in this subject here, the reader needs to be aware that there can be arguments, by clever lawyers, over the validity of an arbitration clause in a contract.

The urge to force people and companies to arbitrate, rather than sue, is so great, nowadays, that the courts will often not even entertain a motion, for any reason, in a case that was marked for arbitration. They will refer all issues to the arbitrator.

But, sometimes, the claims made about the arbitration proceedings are very serious, such as bribery, or bias in the arbitrator or in the panel deciding the arbitration itself. In that event, your attorney, or your adversary's, may try to drag the case into the courts anyway, thereby thwarting the arbitration clause. It's rare, but be aware that it can happen.

THE KEY CONCEPT: BINDING OR NON-BINDING

When drafting a contract, or when agreeing to arbitration, the parties have a choice: should the resulting arbitration be binding, and end the legal dispute forever, or should there be a right of a re-trial, or some kind of appeal?

This is crucial, with competing interests for each position. On the one hand, you might want to appeal, if you lose the case, but feel the arbitrator made a mistake. Then again, if the proceeding is binding, you have the certainty of knowing that, on the day of the arbitration decision, you and your company will finally put this particular dispute behind you, one way or another. That sureness can secure a company's future.

MEDIATION

Mediation is always non-binding. It is merely a conference about the dispute, with one impartial person (the "mediator") discussing it with the parties.

Now, you would think such a proceeding would not have much value. Being a litigator, your narrator always looked down on this kind of proceeding. I was a fan of how the power dynamic shifted when a trial started. Attorneys who exaggerated, and got by with verbose posturing and long speeches, usually got killed by juries.

In a personal sense, all that changed in 2004, in White Plains. My firm had a serious motorcycle case we had been trying to settle for years. Our client had been riding his motorcycle in May of 2000, when he was struck by a car making a U turn on White Plains Road, in the Bronx. The car ran over our client once, then backed up and ran over him again, then drove away.

There were issues with the proper identity of the vehicle and driver. We figured an expensive, risky trial was in our future. The client survived, but his injuries were very bad. We could win big, but we could also lose the whole thing. My partner wanted to try mediation, but I thought it was a waste of time. Eventually, I was convinced, and we arrived at a retired judge's office for the meeting. To kill two birds with one stone, I had some trial exhibits made of the scene of the accident, and of my client's gruesome injuries. We brought an easel with us and set up the big pictures on it. The message I wanted to send was that we were already 'way ahead of them, and seriously prepared to go to trial.

The retired judge practically knocked everyone's heads together. He spoke with us alone first. We demanded $3.5 to settle the case. The mediator immediately convinced us that our case probably wasn't worth as much as we thought.

Then he worked on our adversaries. He got them to make us a substantial offer, which we rejected.

Eventually, working on one side, then the other, he got us closer and closer. Finally, the defendants' representatives made a $1.3 million offer and we called the client from the mediator's office. I was shocked when he accepted it, on the spot, and the case was settled.

Since then, I have been more aware of big cases being settled this way. It shows that a talented mediator can be worth his or her weight in gold!

SUMMARY TRIALS

Although this is a recent concept in our courts, the reader should be aware that this is just another attempt at streamlining the system in a long and tortured history of reform.

Summary trials go by different names. They are sometimes called "minitrials," or summary jury trials (SJT's). Basically, they are binding, one day trials, in which the rules of evidence are somewhat relaxed, and the parties can produce accident and medical reports instead of live, very expensive witnesses.

Other rules generally apply, although they can vary from state to state. We did these trials in the Bronx. You usually can't win by motion in such a trial. If a jury was selected, you must take the verdict. The parties are usually strongly urged (nearly forced) to stipulate (agree on) as many issues as they can before the summary trial.

REFERRALS TO FACT FINDERS, REFEREES OR MAGISTRATES

Another tool in the court's toolbox for alternative dispute resolution is the hand off. As in football, the judge hands part of the case off to someone else to figure out. Usually it will be another judge, a retired lawyer, or a "fact-finder." They will concentrate on one aspect, or issue, in the dispute. The theory is that an unbiased third person can look at some part of the legal action and provide a fresh perspective. Then report back to the court about it.

A referee is often called upon to actually decide a portion of the case. They can accept reports, take testimony and other evidence, and hear motions. Once they make a decision, that is usually binding in the main litigation.

4. INTRODUCTION TO TORTS

Tort law impacts directly on American business on a daily basis. It is so important that professionals and manufacturers have, at times, ceased their business activities until they could get favorable tort law reforms passed.

There has been a constant attempt by lawmakers and courts to sort human conduct into specific categories. A certain set of actions, or elements, constitute an assault, or a battery. Another set of elements indicates negligence. The long history of torts has also generated additional, important special doctrines in tort law, which can trip up the modern manager.

TORT?

In legal terms, a tort is simply a "wrong" against a person or a company, for which there can be a legal remedy. By contrast, a crime is thought to injure our society. Usually, the victim of a tort can sue the person, or firm, that injured him or her, directly. Whereas, a crime is prosecuted by a district attorney, on behalf of all the people that live in the state.

FOUR ELEMENTS

All torts break down into four basic elements. Some torts may concern a person's reputation. Others are about stealing or bodily injury. Nevertheless, they all come down to four things: the (1) breach of some kind of (2) duty or obligation which (3) causes an (4) injury.

Since many torts result in injury, your narrator tried to come up with an appropriate mnemonic aid to help remember these four elements. The word "O.U.C.H." can help you remember what is needed to be proven for conduct to be considered a tort. The letter O is for the obligation which is somehow breached. For instance, in driving, there is an obligation to drive safely. In being an employee, there is an obligation not to steal. The letter U is for unmet. Not meeting the obligation breaches the duty that was owed. So, crashing a car violates the duty to drive it safely. When suing for a tort, it must also be apparent that the unmet obligation is what caused the victim's harm. So, the C is for cause, and the H is for harm.

INTENTIONAL OR NOT? CONSENT OR NOT? PEOPLE OR GOODS?

Private wrongs break down into two kinds, intentional torts and unintentional torts. Based on these categories, the way these torts are treated diverges. Intentional torts usually have short statutes of limitations. Criminal charges, and punitive damages, are often involved with intentional tort claims.

Because intent and consent are often crucial issues in claims against businesses, the need for good records and competent employees should again be obvious.

Most torts concern a person who is the victim of some conduct by the defendant. However, a manager needs to be aware that torts can also be committed against someone's property. Trespass, for example, is a tort that relates to real estate. Conversion concerns stealing property that one is entrusted with. Those will be discussed presently.

TRANSFERRED INTENT

Before we begin to look at these concepts further, we must discuss how intent can be transferred. If a criminal robs a bank with a gun, and tries to shoot a security guard, but misses and hits a bank customer, they cannot avoid blame. In any resulting lawsuit or criminal prosecution, the intent to harm the guard will be automatically transferred to the injured customer.

A celebrated case in this area, loved or hated by baseball fans, is *Manning v. Grimsley*, 643 F.2d 20 (1981). It was September 16, 1975. Ross Grimsley, a pitcher, was warming up in Fenway Park, getting ready to play the Boston Red Sox. It had been a long season, and he hadn't done as well as the year before. The game was crucial, as Boston was in first place, the Orioles in second, and the hated Yankees were in a distant third.

Grimsley was known as a colorful character. He allegedly didn't shower during win streaks, was accused of throwing spitballs by the Yankees' Billy Martin, and had a witch sending him good luck charms. He would have his best year in 1978, when he was selected for the 1978 National League All Star Team. He completed that season with 20 wins and 11 losses, 19 complete games pitched, and a 3.81 ERA.

Fenway is the oldest active stadium in the major leagues. It was built in 1912, and is tiny compared to the huge arenas of today. As a result, Grimsley was throwing his warm up pitches that day very close to the fans in the seats. Boston fans are never quiet, so, the heckling from the right field bleacher creatures started immediately, and continued during the game. Finally, at the end of the third inning, Mr. Grimsley made believe he was going to warm up again, but instead of throwing to his catcher, the ball, going 80 miles per hour, shot right toward the hecklers.

Now, in his defense, he was probably just trying to scare the Boston fans. There was a metal mesh fence protecting the crowd, but the ball went right through it, and hit, and injured, Mr. Manning. The plaintiff brought suit in the federal courts, alleging diversity (i.e., the plaintiff and defendants were from different states). Several witnesses were called. Mr. Grimsley's intent to hit a heckler was legally transferred to the injured baseball fan, and he lost the case.

ASSAULT

Assault is an intentional tort that is sometimes committed by a business through its employees. There is an obligation on us all not to injure people by threatening or frightening them. So the specific elements of an assault include (1) an intentional (2) threat of harm to a person that they can see and appreciate. If your frustrated employee raises a hand to smack an impudent teen customer across the face, that is an assault.

No actual touching is required. The raising of the hand is the assault. The fright from the imminent harm is the heart of the claim, and that is what the jury might award money for. There are some interesting wrinkles. If the teen does not see the upraised hand, there is no tort. If the teen is behind a thick glass door, so the victim's apprehension is not reasonable, then, again, there is no tort committed.

BATTERY

This tort is again connected to the idea that there is a general obligation not to injure others. A battery is any unauthorized, intentional touching that results in upset, or injury. So, a punch in the face is a battery, and so is getting sexually molested in a crowded subway car. Furthermore, direct touching items closely connected with a person can also be a battery. Knocking a person's hat off, or repeatedly kicking their chair, can constitute a battery.

To an extent, a person can consent to being battered. Medical treatment, theatrical performances, and party tricks with drinks can all result in some injury, but be consented to. However, no one can legally consent to be seriously injured.

"ASSAULT AND BATTERY" - DON'T GET CONFUSED

The assault and battery we are discussing above are separate torts. They are not criminal charges. These torts would result in civil (not criminal) litigation between the parties involved. Each party would usually have their own lawyer. The district attorney would not be involved.

However, there is a crime with a very similar sounding name. "Assault and battery" is a criminal charge, for which a person would be arrested, photographed and fingerprinted. It is often used in domestic violence cases. If the police are called, and one spouse has a visible injury, and states that the other spouse caused it, the officers are usually required, by policy, to arrest the person who allegedly caused the visible injury.

As mentioned above, a person cannot validly grant consent to be a victim of the of crime of assault and battery, if it results in serious injury. So, even in the rare cases where victims specifically ask to be hit, or punished, or tell the police that their injury was deserved, the defendant can still be prosecuted for this crime.

So, assault and battery is a criminal charge, but civil assault and civil battery are separate torts, which result in a civil lawsuit.

CRIMES AND TORTS ARE OFTEN RELATED

This brings us to another important idea. Crimes and torts are often committed at the same time. When a robber shoots his or her victim, multiple crimes and torts are committed in the same instant. The shooting is an attempted murder, an aggravated robbery, and an assault with a deadly weapon. But as the gun is aimed, that is a civil assault, when the bullet strikes, a battery claim for personal injuries is created. Other torts will apply also.

Different statutes of limitations will apply to each crime and tort claim. Different standards of proof will apply in the criminal and civil trials. But all the claims and defenses to both the torts and the crimes, will arise in those critical moments.

In cases where a crime and tort were committed simultaneously, usually the victim(s) will want the criminal proceeding to finish before beginning any tort trial. This is because, if there is a criminal conviction, the tort case will be much easier to win.

HOW CAN MY COMPANY BE RESPONSIBLE?

An employer is responsible for the acts of its employees. Normally this means that a worker can enter contracts for the business. But, a business can also be found responsible for an assault, or a battery, by one of its employees. Usually, the key issue in such cases is: "Was the employee acting within the scope of his or her employment at the time of the tort?"

You can never tell where the evidence in these cases will lead. Sometimes the proof will show that the employee assaulted a person while trying to get them to do something to benefit the business. Such an assault may be found to be "in the course of employment," by a jury. That would make the business responsible.

But if the proof shows the employee began beating up the person due to personal reasons, the company will usually not be liable.

SOME PEOPLE HAVE NOTHING TO LOSE

People who commit crimes are often "judgment proof." That means they own nothing. Judgments cannot be enforced against someone with absolutely no legally reachable assets. So plaintiff's attorneys are going to be constantly watching for circumstances in which they can ensnare your company into the litigation, as a "deep pocket" with money, or insurance coverage, that can be tapped.

FALSE IMPRISONMENT

False imprisonment is a tort that businesses usually run afoul of in shoplifting situations. The elements of this tort are nearly universal in America. Your author has created a mnemonic to help remember them. If you can remember the word J.A.I.L., you can remember the elements.

First, there must be some kind of "jail." Now, it doesn't have to be much to result in a lawsuit. Any locked room, or an area with blocked exits, can constitute a jail. It can be temporary. Even if it's just, say, a few burly security guards, standing around the victim, not even touching him or her. If the victim can later convince a judge or jury that they formed a scary barrier, the guards could be committing the tort of false imprisonment. So, in each case, there has to be some kind of confinement of the plaintiff.

Secondly, the confinement must be "against" the law. In other words, a store owner may ask a customer a few questions before they leave, but to be false imprisonment, the circumstances must become unreasonable. Ordering the customer around, locking them in a room, guarding them so they cannot leave or holding them for hours, are all actions that are not supported by current local business statutes. So all those actions, if the person is not guilty of a crime, are all technically against the law and can satisfy an element of the lawsuit.

The I in J.A.I.L. is for intentional. This is an intentional tort, so accidentally locking someone in an office is careless, but, if it is truly accidental, it cannot be false imprisonment. So, whatever is done, the surrounding of the person, holding them somewhere, etc., all must be done on purpose.

Lastly, the defendant, the person or company committing the tort, must lack (the L in J.A.I.L.) the consent of the victim. This is where, believe it or not, a lot of people lose their case in court! If a manager asks a customer if they would mind stepping into his, or her, office to check their receipt, and the customer replies, "Of course. No problem." Well then, there's no lawsuit. The victim has to be imprisoned against their will, not agree to it. Normally, the law leans toward litigants who are polite and patient. Not here. If a customer says they are pressed for time, or that they are suspicious of the employee's motives, that means the customer is not consenting and the situation can escalate into a problem for the firm.

MERCHANT PROTECTION LAWS

There have been so many false imprisonment suits over the years that most states have passed statutes to allow a business owner who suspects someone of stealing, to peacefully stop a customer and do a brief investigation. The emphasis in these laws is being reasonable. If the business owner is reasonable, if the time detained is reasonable, if the person was dealt with calmly, then there is no tort.

Although the real world is a chaotic place, there is a little legal logic at work in the system here. If you meticulously obey the business protection laws, you won't commit the tort of false imprisonment. But, if, as a company, you act cavalierly with regard to the protection statutes, and fail to behave reasonably, you probably will commit the tort.

DON'T EXCEED LEGAL AUTHORITY TRYING TO PROTECT THE COMPANY

In law, there seems to be a constant pendulum, with legal trends that sway one way, then the other. Sometimes companies go too far, trying to protect themselves. In 2016, Macy's was ordered, by a Manhattan judge, to stop having suspected shoplifters sign confessions and pay damages before being released.

State Supreme Court Justice Manuel Mendez said that the company had no legal authority to act as a police force, especially since the victims had no right to counsel nor a hearing. The judge issued an injunction. An injunction is a valid, formal court order to stop doing something, usually immediately. They are often used, sometimes without effect, during labor disputes and strikes.

The attorney for the customers said that Macy's was detaining young, mostly minority patrons, who were bullied into signing confessions. They would then be arrested, besides. Ross, Barbara. "Macy's Can't Shop." *N.Y. Daily News*, 30 June, 2016, p. 97.

DEFAMATION

Defamation is (1) intentionally making (2) an untrue statement (oral or written) about somebody which then (3) injures their reputation and/or their ability to make money.

Notice, again, the key elements of intent and damage. The defendant must know that their statement is a lie. One cannot accidentally defame someone.

Another wrinkle in this tort is that statements that are opinions are not actionable. So, "John has AIDS," is defamatory, if untrue, but, "I think John acts stupid," is not.

TWO FLAVORS

Defamation comes into your business life in one of two ways. Slander is oral defamation. 'Defamation by spoken word. If you, or your employee, say something untrue about another, and that person finds out, you can face some exposure for this tort. On the other hand, when someone makes an untrue oral statement about you or your employees, you may have a claim.

The other flavor is called libel. The elements are the same as slander, but in writing. This area of defamation, because of the western world's preoccupation with celebrities, has had a lot more litigation in recent years. Johnny Depp, Sean Penn, Tom Cruise, Scarlett Johansson, Cameron Diaz, Donald Trump, Sharon Stone, Brad Pitt, Angelina Jolie, Kate Hudson, and

Shakira (to name but a few) have all brought actions involving defamation in some way.

The zealousness of our print media in the U.S. has caused so many written defamation suits, that the law has been well developed, here. Our courts have repeatedly affirmed the principle that, due to the way American industry and media are structured, celebrities intentionally and repeatedly seek publicity to advance their careers. Therefore, they cannot have the same level of protection from defamation that a person receives when they intentionally keep their life private.

The result is that, if it can be proven that you are a celebrity, you must prove the usual elements of the tort, like anyone else. But you must also prove that any written defamation was done with "actual malice." Actual malice is defined as writing something that was a lie, or writing something recklessly, in complete disregard for whether it was true or not. *N.Y. Times v Sullivan*, 376 U.S. 254 (1964).

VIOLATION OF THE RIGHT TO PUBLICITY

In America, movie stars have been discovered running along a beach, or working at a drug store. It doesn't matter how hideous a person looks, millions of dollars can be made if your face is picked out of the crowd for a fast food ad campaign. No one can tell you how to cash in on this right. But every one of us possesses it. It's called your right to publicity.

Your face, how you talk, how you move, are all uniquely your own. They can be incorporated into a character or a cartoon. However, if anyone utilizes your likeness, and makes money, you are supposed to get paid.

In the case of *White v. Samsung Elecs. Am., Inc.*, 989 F.2d 1512 (9th Cir. 1993), celebrity Vanna White sued the gigantic Samsung Electronics Company over a commercial they made and aired. The TV ad showed a robot, that looked like her, turning letters in the future. The idea was that Samsung's products were well made and lasted a long time. After Vanna White sued, the judge in the case held that, because Samsung didn't actually use her name, voice or signature, it didn't violate her right of publicity. Vanna White appealed and won. At a later trial, she was awarded $403,000.00 in damages.

These disputes still occur. Ariana Grande sued Forever 21 and a company called Riley Rose in 2019, in California, claiming they published unauthorized pictures and videos of her, to create a false impression that she endorsed their products. Sblendorio, Peter. "Ariana Hits Ad 'Double.'" *N.Y. Daily News*, 4 Sept., 2019, p. 3. Obviously, this tort is alive and well in America, today.

THE RIGHT TO PRIVACY

There is an additional tort that is rarely involved in litigation, at least during your author's career. However, it can be an important method of redress for everyday people whose privacy is violated. The cause of action for violation of the right to privacy is similar to defamation, but the facts publicized do not need to be false. This is crucial to the claim.

Each of us possesses a right to privacy. It's sometimes referred to as the right to be left alone. We don't want everyone to know what medical conditions we have. Most people don't want others to know about legal, or emotional, problems they had in the past. This is especially so in the case of non-celebrities, who have never intentionally promoted themselves in the media.

Therefore, there is a duty to not to intentionally reveal intimate facts about others which could damage them. If someone reveals private facts about a person's life, and that person is not a celebrity, the one doing the revealing can be sued for invasion of privacy. This is so, even if the facts revealed are absolutely and completely true. Of course, as with all torts, there has to be real damages that result.

One caveat is that private people can become unfortunate celebrities without their consent. If a person witnesses a famous event, or is involved in something newsworthy, they can lose their private status in the eyes of the law, and become a person of interest to the public. It must be understood that there is never a declaration that "so and so lost his private status today." Instead, a person will sue, based on the right of privacy, and the jury will tell them, with its verdict, that they lost because they are a public figure now.

A WORD ABOUT "CODIFICATION"

The right of privacy, mentioned above, came to us through various sections of the U.S. Constitution, but also from the English "common law."

That common law is based on years of similar individual cases going through the courts, and forming a body of law in various areas of tort law. It continues down to the present day. Individual cases still create a lot of new law in America each year.

When new cases are reported, lawmakers around the country study them to see if there is a need for legislation on the same legal matters. The more controversial, difficult and sensational an individual case is, the more attention it will get as to needed legislation. In this way, many legal precedents, based on actual cases, have been "codified," or re-written, as formal, written laws.

The right of privacy, in the area of a person's medical history, has been codified in the well known Health Insurance Portability and Accountability Act (HIPAA). This federal statute was passed in 1996 and generally outlines the right of privacy with regard to a person's medical information. It covers everyone in the United States, and can result in civil or criminal prosecution. The Department of Health and Human Services' Office for Civil Rights can fine violators.

In this area we can see how the common law works together with codified law. Any litigant who has had their medical information improperly revealed, will cite the violation of privacy common law in their complaint. Then, they will go on to also allege "a violation of the HIPAA Statute," either as evidence that their privacy was, indeed, violated, or as a second, separate violation claim entirely.

INTENTIONAL INFLICTION OF EMOTIONAL DISTRESS

The tort of intentional infliction of emotional distress is more common that many people think, and the elements of this tort are straightforward and simple. A party who experiences intentional, terrible conduct by another that causes them real, severe mental distress, may bring an action for money damages.

The two misconceptions the public seems to have about such claims are that (1) any bothersome or nasty activity can be the basis for such a lawsuit, and (2) the party suing can easily prove mental distress.

The actionable conduct has to be really out of the bounds of normal behavior. In their opinions over the years, judges have used the words "outrageous" "intolerable" and "atrocious" to characterize the kind of actions this tort guards against.

So, teasing you about your haircut is not tortious conduct. Neither is repeatedly frightening you when you come home from work each night. That may be harassment, or some other tort, but it's not intentional infliction of emotional distress.

Intentionally hiding someone's child, calling a person racial names, ridiculing their poor health, repeatedly seriously threatening to attack, are all examples of behavior that might constitute inflicting mental distress on another.

The tort is more common than you might think because it often arises as a second claim in lawsuits involving intentional torts. So, in lawsuits alleging sex discrimination, or false imprisonment, the plaintiff will also claim intentional infliction of emotional distress. That way, they can win on either, or both, of their claims.

The other area people seem to be confused about this tort is concerning the damages. Sometimes, a lawyer will be lucky enough to receive an easy "intentional infliction case" where his client had no prior mental issues, and started extensive psych treatment right after the incident. But, that's rare. Most people's lives are not as neatly packaged as that. In actuality, it can be somewhat difficult to prove mental damages were caused directly by a specific incident or actions.

Permanent damages can be important in these cases. But, when a party suffers an emotional distress, they cannot come into court and simply testify that "now I'm afraid of dogs" or "I can't travel on planes." This tort is really geared to serious, long term claims, provable by medical records and doctors. If a litigant cannot provide that proof, their claim can be dismissed, or narrowed by the court, during pre-trial motion practice, before the trial has even started.

The result is a very expensive, complex proceeding. Expert witnesses and voluminous records are usually needed to convince the judge, and jury, to award a substantial verdict in the plaintiff's favor, based on this tort. Run-of-the-mill tort lawyers hate these kinds of cases. They are expensive and take a lot of work. The victim often has to first convince his or her own attorney to take the case on.

Another downside of any mental distress claim is that the defendant's attorney is free to delve into the plaintiff's past, and make the most of any disorders, or prior psych treatment the plaintiff experienced before the incident in question. People make mental distress claims, only to have an extensive history of pre-existing mental illness be discovered by the defense's investigators. Unless the claimant has a very sharp lawyer, such a trial can become a truly awful proceeding.

THE *ROACH* CASE

A famous case in this area is *Roach v Stern*, 675 N.Y.S.2d 133 (1998). Deborah Roach, known as "Debbie Tay," was a topless dancer and a frequent guest on Howard Stern's radio show. In April of 1995, she died of a heroin overdose. Her sister, Melissa Roach, had Deborah cremated and gave some of her remains to Chaunce Hayden, who had been a friend of her sister's. On July 18, 1995, Hayden appeared on Stern's show, which was also videotaped. He brought a box with the woman's remains with him. The show personnel then proceeded to shake, handle and joke around with the burnt fragments of the corpse. They said things like: "That's her head, that's a piece of her teeth" and "That's a rib? Oh yeah, wow, she was a piece."

The family heard the broadcast and sued for intentional infliction of emotional distress in Brooklyn Supreme Court. Howard Stern won the first round. Kings County Judge Richard D. Huttner found that the defendants' conduct was not "beyond all bounds of decency." So, it was not outrageous enough for him, and he threw the case out. However, the plaintiffs appealed his ruling, and won. Several years ago, while researching the case in the New York State Court records, after that appeal, your author could not find any more proceedings in the case. We assume the parties did what 97% of litigants do, and they entered into a settlement agreement. The defendants may have "seen the writing on the wall," and felt they might lose. Plus, the bad publicity of a trial could have a negative impact on their careers. So, ending the case was in their best interests. On the other hand, the plaintiffs probably wanted to make a point, rather than make a lot of money, or drag celebrities through the mud. They also might not have been looking forward to an expensive, lengthy, public trial. These are some of the practical reasons cases get settled.

It seems obvious that there was a non-disclosure agreement (more about that, later) as to the settlement terms, which covered comments by both sides, as nothing else was ever heard from them about this, in print nor on the air.

INTENTIONAL TORTS AGAINST PROPERTY

Thus far, we have discussed wrongs committed against people. However, as we mentioned at the start of this chapter, torts can also be thought of as being committed against property. The money damages, in any resulting lawsuit, go to the owner of the property, but these are still classified as "torts against property." As previously mentioned in chapter 2, there are only two kinds of property for legal purposes, (1) real estate and (2) everything else ("personal property").

TRESPASSING ON LAND

Everyone knows about trespassing, right? You're not allowed to trespass. Sometimes you see signs: "No trespassing! This means you!" They can also say "Authorized Entry Only," or some other phrase. The meaning is clear: stay out!

Trespassing is going on someone else's land. Well, no, it's actually not that simple. There are lots of little wrinkles in this old English common law tort from the thirteenth century.

If someone cuts across your yard every day, as you have coffee on your front porch, that is technically a trespass to land, but most attorneys would probably advise you not to sue. That's because you have no real damages. The trespasser is not injuring your property.

Surprisingly, in this simple example, the legal obligation, in our modern world, seems to be on the landowner. It is really up to the property owner to do something. They can put up a fence, buy a dog or take some other action. But, whatever they do, it must be safe, and not injure the trespasser, nor anyone else.

Again, we are dealing here with a civil tort, not the crime of criminal trespass. Criminal trespass requires "knowledge," so it's basically remaining on land even though you surely know you're not supposed to be there, like blocking a road or walking on a runway.

Note the elements present in civil trespass. There is (1) an obligation, on each of us, to stay off private property. It is our responsibility to know where we are. So we cannot claim, "I did not know" in a simple, civil trespass case. In addition, the tort requires only the defendant's (2) intentional breach of that obligation, by simply walking onto the property, then (3) causing (4) damage.

Damages? Walking through a flower bed would injure the land, and it would also slightly lower its value. That's a valid claim of damage. If someone pitches a tent and starts living on your property, you can't use that area of your land anymore. You have sustained a provable "loss of use." That is also a valid claim of damage, due to trespass.

TRESPASS TO PROPERTY

Whenever someone takes or damages someone else's stuff, they commit the tort of trespass to property. The key element is the intentional interference with the ownership rights the plaintiff has with regard to a particular piece, or pieces, of personal property. Back in the day, it was originally called "trespass to chattels," chattels being another term for personal property.

CONVERSION

Closely related to trespass to property is the tort of conversion, which occurs in two ways. First, when a person simply takes something of yours, or something belonging to your company, and uses it for themselves. It can be cash, an animal, a car, anything. If they get it somehow, they improperly "converted" that personal property from your use, or your company's use, to theirs, and, if you find out, they can be sued.

The other form of conversion is more common. Instead of outright theft, the plaintiff entrusts her or his property to the defendant. Then, abusing that trust, the tortfeasor (the one committing the tort) converts the property to their own use. So, when an employee steals company supplies or submits fake expense receipts, they are converting their employers' property, and would be liable in a civil suit, regardless of what other laws those same acts may violate.

HOW DOES THIS ACTUALLY HAPPEN IN BUSINESS?

Right about now, one may ask, how does all this go down in the real world? What do I do if I discover conversion by my employee? What really happens? Well, one of the most common scenarios is when someone in the office finds out that a company they've been paying is either fake, or somehow connected with an employee of the firm. A further investigation sometimes reveals that an executive, or high level clerk, entrusted with the power to pay for services billed to his employer, was having gambling problems, or marital problems or a drug issue. The dishonest employee created a fake corporation, then paid it for work that was never done, and collected the cash at their local bank.

Usually, what happens is the company calls in its legal department or retains an attorney experienced in business law. Key issues are: how much evidence is there? Must the employee be stopped immediately to prevent further damage to the company? The attorney may then bring the evidence of the conduct to the local county district attorney, to see if criminal charges are warranted. There may be an arrest. Depending on the circumstances and the personalities involved there might be a meeting with the defendant to discuss a settlement to avoid prosecution. Usually, corporations just want to get their money back and sack the worker and quietly move on, without adverse publicity. If an agreement can't be reached, the company's lawyer files a civil suit for conversion, embezzlement, fraud and theft, and we're off to the races. That's how it's done.

5. NEGLIGENCE AND UNINTENTIONAL TORTS

Negligence is "The King of the Courtroom," nowadays. There is a tremendous amount of personal injury and property damage litigation, based on negligence, in the United States, each year. There have been repeated reforms, over decades, to curb the amount and scope of negligence lawsuits. Some progress has been made. But such cases still clog our courts.

This tort is based on the ancient English common law obligation to exercise due care in everything we do. When operating machines, doing labor, and in our leisure activities, we need to be careful to avoid injuring others or damaging their property. Hand in hand with this idea is the concept that accidents usually happen when people are careless.

A SYSTEM BASED ON FAULT

So what was created was a litigation system, based on fault. In these cases, where someone is careless, and unintentionally injures a plaintiff, the defendant is said to be "at fault," and therefore can be held liable for money damages. However, sometimes accidents happen, even when we can prove that we were being very careful. In those cases, a defendant would be less responsible, or not responsible at all.

ELEMENTS

Each negligence case causes a search for its four elements. So, in any fact pattern one is given, we will look first for an obligation on the proposed defendant. These duties come in a tremendous variety of forms. So, remember, there is an obligation to drive safely, to take care of children, don't knock anyone over, don't poison anyone, don't give out wrong information, be careful at work and generally don't injure anyone, or damage anything, while going about your everyday life.

Once we find an obligation, we search for our second element, a breach of that duty. Over the years, industrialization occurred in the western world, and travel became more popular. The nature of the duties people and firms owed to their customers began to change.

For example, firms that provide public transportation have a higher duty to the public than others. The reason is that, when we ride a bus or a commuter railroad, most of us are unaware how to drive the thing, nor how the emergency door mechanisms work. Meanwhile, there may be all sorts of hazards (fumes, electric shock, operator qualifications) that we may not even know about. So the bus company and the railroad has a higher duty than your friend driving you to work in their car. Hotels also have a higher duty to keep you safe, because you are totally dependent on them for your safety in a very unfamiliar environment.

FORESEEABILITY AND THE "REASONABLE HUMAN"

Foreseeability, and the "imaginary reasonable person" concept, enter business law here. In negligence cases, when juries are ultimately asked to reach a verdict concerning a company's conduct, they will look at whether the accident was foreseeable. The jury's logic often (but not always) goes like this: "If the company was acting reasonably, and the accident was not foreseeable, then it was impossible for the firm to prevent what happened. Therefore, the incident was not the company's fault."

On the other hand, if the company was blind to foreseeable danger, and was not "acting as a reasonable person would," to correct the hazard, then the company could have prevented the incident, and is therefore responsible for any direct injuries that resulted.

PROXIMATE CAUSE

Cause is the third element in negligence cases. If there was an obligation and a breach, then one must determine if the breach of the duty is what caused the plaintiff's injury. At this point, we must briefly discuss the famous case of *Palsgraf v. Long Island Railroad Co.*, 248 N.Y. 339 (1928). How this lawsuit became a leading case for determining proximate cause is impossible to determine.

The facts, to this day, are crazy. Helen Palsgraf was waiting for a train at a station on Long Island. In those days, they had large, coin operated scales on the platform. They were used to weigh baggage and freight, to determine the cost of a ticket. A train came into the station, and a man ran to catch it. As he got on, a conductor helped him and the man dropped a package. Incredibly, it exploded very forcefully! The whole platform shook, and the scale fell over and hit poor Helen. The case made it all the way to the highest New York State court, the Court of Appeals, in Albany. The court held that her injury was not foreseeable under the circumstances and the railroad had not caused her injury.

In law school we were solemnly told, repeatedly, that, after we graduated, this case would act as our standard as to whether causation existed in our negligence cases. When I was finally in practice, I found myself asking clients, "Nothing exploded and knocked something over in your case?" In over thirty years of litigation experience I never had a case like *Palsgraf*, nor could I ever figure out how this case was supposed to help me determine proximate cause of a litigant's injury when my clients fell, or were injured in car accidents.

As your author gained experience, I grew to prefer the definition of "cause" contained in the instructions the judges gave to the jury at the end of the evidence phase of a trial. I urge the reader to do the same. Some action or conduct is the proximate cause of an event if it was "a substantial factor" in bringing it about. It has to be the near cause, the direct cause, not something indirect, or remote or trivial.

INJURY

Lastly, there has to be a real injury. Again, this area has been the target of numerous reforms. In New York, we have adopted a no-fault system for claimants injured in car accidents. Medical expenses and lost wages are covered by the insurance carrier of the vehicle the person was riding in, regardless of who caused the accident. The only remaining personal injury issues would be pain and suffering, and permanence. To limit frivolous litigation, state law prevents anyone from suing unless they sustained a "serious injury." A serious injury is then defined, by a rambling, confusing statute, to include things like permanent scars, fractured bones, loss of a limb, or the loss of use of a bodily system. The takeaway is that a real, substantial injury is the final element in a negligence case.

STELLA LIEBECK

Liebeck v. McDonald's Restaurants, P.T.S., Inc., No. D-202 CV-93-02419, 1995, has been extensively studied because it demonstrates, with incredibly memorable facts, many of the routine aspects of the court system's operation with regard to torts: There is an awful accident. Medics pick up the pieces. The victim experiences some unexpected expenses, maybe loses time from work. A preliminary call or letter is sent, or a formal insurance claim is made with the carrier of the possible defendant. There are some preliminary negotiations. In time, there's an outright demand for some money and, maybe, a small (often, insulting) offer in return. The parties fail to agree. Attorneys are retained. The positions of the parties harden even more. Investigators start sniffing around, taking pictures and interviewing witnesses. Eventually, litigation begins.

It was February 27, 1992, and she was 79 years old, as her grandson drove his 1989 Ford Probe into a McDonald's at 5001 Gibson Boulevard Southeast in Albuquerque, New Mexico. She got a cup of coffee. The car was stopped as she put the hot coffee between her knees to hold it steady, in order to add cream and sugar. As she pulled the cup lid backward, the entire cup of coffee spilled into her lap. She suffered third degree burns, lost 20% of her body weight, was hospitalized for eight days and received skin grafts. She was pretty much totally disabled for about two years.

At first, the injured woman just tried to convince McDonald's to pay her $20,000.00 to cover some of her expenses. The company offered her $800.00. Such a low offer in response to a demand is called "low balling," in the industry.

Stella went and got herself a good lawyer. She retained Reed Morgan, of Texas. He filed suit in New Mexico, and accused McDonald's of gross negligence, in that they sold coffee that was "unreasonably dangerous" and "defectively manufactured".

McDonald's refused Morgan's offer to settle for $90,000.00. After months of getting the case prepared for trial, and paying his expert witnesses, the plaintiff's settlement demand went up considerably. Morgan demanded $300,000.00 to settle, one last time. A mediation was arranged, and the mediator suggested a $225,000.00 settlement, just before trial. McDonald's refused and jury selection commenced.

A twelve-person jury reached a verdict on August 18, 1994. They found that McDonald's was 80% responsible and Liebeck was 20% negligent herself. There was a warning on the coffee cup about the danger, but the jury found that the warning was not sufficient. They awarded Liebeck $200,000.00 in compensatory damages, which was reduced by her 20% fault to $160,000.00.

In addition, and this is crucial, they awarded her $2.7 million for punitive damages, to punish McDonald's and make it an example to other fast food companies.

The key to understanding the jury's verdict is the evidence they heard about that coffee. The jury heard, through expert testimony, that the coffee was close to 190 degrees F. That's only 22 degrees below the boiling point of water! Nobody else in the surrounding area served coffee that hot. About 70 people a year scalded themselves with McDonald's coffee. Some claims had been settled by McDonald's for hundreds of thousands of dollars.

The trial judge felt that the punitive damages award was too high and reduced it to $480,000, three times the compensatory amount, which is a "traditional" multiplier often used for such damages. The total plaintiff's verdict was $640,000.00.

Amazingly, the parties had not had enough yet! The verdict, and the court's decisions were appealed by both sides. But the parties eventually settled out of court, for an undisclosed amount.

On the one hand the case is considered the height of stupidity and an example of the ridiculous laws companies have to contend with in the United States. Others see it as a good example of how a modern tort case should go. The coffee was far too hot and the plaintiff was seriously injured.

LIABILITY WITHOUT FORESEEING WHAT MIGHT HAPPEN

We now know that foreseeability is very important in negligence cases. But a firm can be held responsible for a tort, even if the precise injury that occurs was not foreseeable. If the company's carelessness caused the risk of injury, it will be legally responsible for the results. *Fischer v. Pepsi*, 972 F.2d 906 (1992) demonstrates this doctrine.

Robert J. Fischer was a guest at a Red Lion Inn in Omaha, Nebraska, in 1987. He went swimming, and then approached an electric soda vending machine. What he didn't know was that, due to lousy maintenance, wiring insulation had worn away on the main power wire. The bare copper wire, with electricity running through it, was in contact with the metal exterior cabinet of the machine. Still wet, when he inserted money in the machine, Mr. Fischer received a substantial electric shock. He reported the incident, and later began having pain during sex with his wife. He eventually sued Pepsi.

The plaintiff won the case at trial and he was awarded $324,000.00 by the jury. In 1987, that was a substantial sum, and Pepsi appealed. On the appeal, the whole case turned on these questions: Was what happened foreseeable? Did Pepsi have to foresee exactly what happened, or just know that there was some danger?

The appellate court affirmed the jury's verdict. The court stated that "It is unnecessary that the particular injury or precise form of the injury be perceived or foreseen." The appeals court also wrote that, if the plaintiff proved there was a hazard that a reasonable person would correct, then the defendant would be liable. The evidence in the case showed that Pepsi, through its employees, knew of problems like this with their machines. Over time, nothing had been done to maintain the machines, to prevent electric shocks, especially near pools.

So, be warned. Employees need to be instructed to correct problems and hazards they observe that are under the company's control. This is true even if exact accident scenarios can't be specifically identified.

EXPERT WITNESSES

A separate issue in the *Fischer* case was, how did the jury connect the electric shock with the impotence, and then arrive at the figure of $324,000.00? This was result of expert medical/legal testimony.

There is a large, multimillion dollar industry in America that supplies expert witnesses to the nation's litigation attorneys. These experts come in all shapes, colors and genders, and they can find people who are qualified to testify on nearly any subject under the sun, in all different kinds of lawsuits.

Do you need to prove a car was speeding before the accident? Then get an accident re-constructionist, and a safety engineer. For an incredibly exorbitant extra fee, your experts will prepare a convincing, totally biased, 3D video reconstruction of what happened. It is guaranteed to put your client in the best light. Do you need to connect your client's injury with the accident? Spend thousands and get a report from an accomplished local specialist. 'You need to prove the value of a future pension? Hire an economist.

So, that's how the jury in the *Fischer* case found probable cause in that amount. Expert testimony helped them.

SINGERS AND THEIR LYRICS

Could a singer be responsible for a suicide? That was the issue in *McCollum v. CBS, Inc.*, 249 Cal. Rptr. 187 (1988). Ozzie Osborne was a recording artist on the CBS label. He had written a song that seemed to actually urge listeners to kill themselves. "Suicide is the only way out," was one lyric.

On October 26, 1984, in California, a troubled 19 year old, named John Daniel McCollum, was repeatedly listening to the Osborne song, "Suicide Solution," with headphones on. Then he shot himself in the head with a .22 caliber pistol.

His parents brought a wrongful death action against CBS and Ozzie Osborne. They alleged negligence in putting out the song, and also liability for intentionally inciting suicide. The trial judge threw the case out, saying the defendants owed no duty to the listener. That eliminated the negligence claim. The court further found that someone actually killing themselves, because of the song, was not reasonably foreseeable, and did not overcome the artist's right of free speech. This was partly because the lyrics were barely understandable. That eliminated any intentional tort.

The trial court's decision was appealed, but the appellate court affirmed the decision. The case was later featured in an episode of VH-1's "Behind the Music." This case was a total pre-trial win, by motion, for the defendants, and a total loss for the plaintiffs.

NEGLIGENT INFLICTION OF EMOTIONAL DISTRESS

We previously saw the tort of intentional infliction of emotional distress. This is the negligence version of that tort.

Growing out of the general obligation to not injure others, there is also a concurrent obligation not to injure others directly in front of their close relatives. It is felt that this is an additional tort, apart from any claims the injured relative has, for which a jury may make a separate award. Nothing makes a plaintiff's attorney happier than to hear that.

The case of *Estrada v. Aeronaves*, 967 F.2d 1421 (1992) was the result of a devastating midair collision between a jet and a small plane above Cerritos, California on August 31, 1986. It is a well known example of a negligent infliction case. After studying the case for years, your narrator was surprised to see a TV program about the accident. It was on the Smithsonian Channel, and the series was called "Air Disasters." The plaintiff was interviewed. It was very dramatic, and brought home the fact that, while we try to objectively discuss these cases, they obviously have terrible consequences for real people.

Theresa Estrada left her house to go shopping. Her husband and children stayed home. In the sky, 6,500 feet above her, an Aeromexico DC-9 jet, with 64 people on board, was gliding down toward Los Angeles International Airport, some 24 miles to the northwest. It was going about 220 mph. The visibility was 14 miles.

At the same time, a small Piper airplane, with a relatively inexperienced pilot, and two passengers, was climbing, going east, at about the same altitude.

The front of the Piper airplane hit the jet in the left side, just under the horizontal portion of the tail, at 80 mph. The roof of the small plane sheared off, and the three people were instantly decapitated. Most of the jet's tail was knocked completely off. The 50 ton airliner, completely out of control, turned upside down, and fell straight down. It crashed right on top of Mrs. Estrada's house, killing most of her immediate family. Mrs. Estrada returned home to find her house on fire.

There was no issue as to her being owed damages, and a jury eventually awarded Mrs. Estrada $5.5 million for the wrongful death of her family. The jury found the private pilot 50% liable, and the air traffic controller, employed by the United States, also 50% liable.

But the sticking point was that part of the verdict was a claim of negligent infliction of emotional distress. The jury had awarded Mrs. Estrada $1 million for that portion of the case, and the government, responsible for at least $500,000.00 of it, appealed.

The government lost. The appellate court held that Mrs. Estrada had properly proved her case to the jury, by establishing each element of the tort. She proved that the (1) defendants negligently caused the crash, then proved that (2) she was directly, and closely, related to the victims, and that she was (3) present at the accident scene and knew exactly what had happened to her family. Lastly, she showed that she (4) suffered real emotional damage.

THE NEW YORK WRINKLE: "ZONE OF DANGER"

New York, unlike California, still has what is called the "Zone of Danger" doctrine relative to the tort of negligent infliction of emotional distress. In New York the plaintiff must have been in the "zone of danger" at the time of the accident. In other words, if the victim sees the occurrence, and was so close to their relative that he or she was also almost killed or injured, then that victim can sue for negligent infliction of mental distress. But, if the accident happened around the corner, and the plaintiff didn't also almost get injured, there is no negligent infliction claim. Like any tort law, this could be overruled in the future. But, currently, there is a disparity between state laws on the subject.

These kind of cases still appear in the media all the time, often involving motor vehicles. For instance, in May of 2016, a 3 year old girl was walking across 164th Street at Gerard Avenue, near Yankee Stadium, in the Bronx. She was 10 feet behind her mother when she was hit and killed by a car that had a green light. Parascandola, Rocco. "Ma 10 ft. in Front of Tot." *N.Y. Daily News*, 18 May, 2016. In September of 2019, another mom was feeding her 20 month old girl in a stroller, on White Plains Road, in the Bronx. An alleged drunken driver jumped the curb and struck the child, killing her. Burke and Annese. "Drunken Driver Jumps Curb." *N.Y. Daily News*, 18 Sept., 2019, p. 4. Those parents were in the zone of danger in those accidents.

MALPRACTICE

This is an area that makes lawyers happy, when they sue others for it, but upset when they are sued for the same thing.

Malpractice is an emotionally charged word. It has been responsible for ruined lives and astronomical verdicts widely reported in the news. But, objectively, malpractice is no different from any other negligence claim. The key is, malpractice is negligence when committed by a professional, while working.

The most common type of malpractice actions today are medical malpractice cases. And that publicity has stirred much debate. American physicians have long claimed that the entire tort and insurance system is unfair to them. On the other hand, the plaintiff's bar associations around the nation seem to agree that the whole system should be simpler, cheaper and broader, allowing more claims, and recoveries in larger amounts.

LAVERN'S LAW

An example of the controversy is Lavern's Law in New York. Lavern Wilkinson was a lady who got a chest x-ray, at a municipal hospital, in 2010, and was told she was fine. She wasn't fine. There had been real errors, and she later discovered she had been totally misdiagnosed. Her lung cancer, treatable at that time, had been "missed."

Normally, if a doctor "missed" something, and a patient didn't find out for a period of time, the patient had 2.5 years, from when he or she found out, to sue. For example, if your current doctor found a scalpel inside you, left by another doctor, during an operation many years ago, you would have 2.5 years from that discovery to sue for medical malpractice.

But Lavern got that x-ray at a municipal hospital. The statute of limitations, for her, was woefully short: just 15 months from the date of "error." She could not sue and died in 2013. Evans, Heidi. "Lavern Wilkinson, Victim Of Medical Malpractice Dies." *N.Y. Daily News*, 7 March, 2013.

New York enacted Lavern's Law in 2018. It extends the statute of limitations in cases where a physician fails to discover cancer and the time limit of 2.5 years runs from the date of the discovery of the misdiagnosis. Dozens of community organizations were for the law. The law was opposed by the "deep pocketed medical establishment, which has argued that many of the states that have similar measures in place also have caps on pain and suffering awards and limits on total damages." Lovett, Kenneth. "Cure This Law." *N.Y. Daily News*, 17 May, 2016. See? Controversial.

THE LAW OF MALPRACTICE

The law behind these cases, whether it's medical, legal or other professional malpractice, is excruciatingly simple. All the liability issues boil down to one question: did the professional fall below the community standard, when working at his or her craft?

But the science involved in "med mal cases," as they're called, can be maddening complex. The media sometimes presents a picture of a competent, consistent medical system, carefully and honestly recording each thing done for the patient, and always making people healthier. When you peel back that public relations campaign, and get deeply involved in medical malpractice claims, you learn that medicine is like any other human endeavor. Costly mistakes are sometimes made, hopefully not often. Crucial records can be lost or manipulated, and human beings can become complacent and careless.

Sometimes the "community standard" of where the treatment was administered can be an issue. The parties in most cases are free to argue to the jury that the standard of medical care was very high in that area at that precise time period (usually the plaintiff's position) or very low (usually the defendant's position).

6. ADDITIONAL NEGLIGENCE CONCEPTS

The history of negligence is a long and winding one. Many different doctrines and concepts have left their unique impression on this tort. Here is just a sampling of some distinctive legal theories that are still accepted law in some states today.

NEGLIGENCE PER SE

This is a very common rule used in negligence lawsuits. It is available to a plaintiff, and sometimes to a defendant, when three things exist in a case: (1) the plaintiff is injured (or sustains property damage) and the other party was not only careless, but (2) violated a written statute, when causing the injury, and (3) the law violated was passed specifically to protect people like the plaintiff. In that case, the defendant is said to be negligent per se, and the only matters in controversy are the percentages of fault and the amount to be awarded.

Speeding is a good example. At the trial of a personal injury suit, due to a car accident, the plaintiff's attorney will often try very hard to prove that the defendant was going over the legal limit, even if it's just by 1 mph, just before the accident. That's because they know that, if the three elements mentioned above are satisfied, a very favorable instruction will be given to the jury about negligence per se.

Let's face it. Plaintiff's lawyers love this doctrine because it stains the defendant with the guilt of the law violator. What juror can resist adding on a few bucks to the verdict to teach a violator a lesson? That would be totally improper, of course. But that's how people on juries think, sometimes, and that's how verdicts get decided.

RES IPSA LOQUITUR

This is another popular concept in American litigation. No one is sure how old this idea is. Some say it goes back to the Romans. Res ipsa loquitur means "the thing speaks for itself." In other words, the way the accident happened indicates negligence. So this doctrine applies in cases where a jet airliner takes off and disappears. A ship departs but is never seen again. A doctor amputates the good leg.

The doctrine came about by necessity. One of its earliest uses was in the English case of *Byrne v Boadle*, 2 Hurl. & Colt. 722 (1863). A barrel of flour rolled out of the second story of a building where Boadle's flour was sold, just as Mr. Byrne was walking by. It hit him right in the head. He sued, but a problem for him emerged. He could not prove how the defendant was negligent. He and his lawyer knew someone had made a mistake, but they could not prove it. The case was dismissed, and they appealed. The appellate court ruled that there were some cases where negligence should be presumed.

Here are the specific elements: (1) The way the injury occurred does not normally happen without carelessness. (2) What caused the injury was in the exclusive control of the defendant.

These cases are still arising today. In 2018 an army vet sued a Veterans Affairs hospital, in Connecticut, because a scalpel was left in him after surgery. Glenford Turner, 61, of Bridgeport, filed suit in federal court. He had prostate surgery in 2013, but experienced pain and dizziness four years later. An x-ray quickly revealed his problem and he had the instrument surgically removed. *VA Left Scalpel Inside Me*, Associated Press, 16 Jan., 2018.

GOOD SAMARITAN LAWS

Back in the 1960's the media and popular culture seemed to begin questioning, seriously, what duties each member of society owed to the general population, if any. Timothy Leary was advocating, no joke, that we all obtain some LSD and "turn on, tune in, and drop out!"

Against this backdrop there were scandals that were played up in the growing mass media industry. Catherine Genovese was stabbed to death, in Queens, New York, and it appeared that some people ignored her, although they heard yelling and some looked out their windows. There were other accounts of atrocious behavior. People who were injured in accidents, turned around and sued health care practitioners that stopped to help them. Then stories emerged about health care professionals who refused to help people in emergencies, for fear of being sued!

The result in America, over the years, has been the widespread use of Good Samaritan Laws. These laws state a specific set of guidelines to protect health care professionals. Nowadays, other laws and programs have adopted the name, so be careful about what exact statutes you're referring to.

New York passed its present Good Samaritan Law, Section 3000-a of the New York Public Health Law, in 1984. It protects medical professionals, and, to some extent, even the general public, when they help someone "at the scene of an accident or other emergency outside of a hospital, doctor's office, or any other place having necessary medical equipment." The statute is surprisingly complex. Nevertheless, it basically makes it hard to sue and win in a civil medical malpractice lawsuit against someone who treats an injured person at the scene of an accident. The nurse or doctor would have to do something reckless, or totally outrageous, to be found liable.

THE NEW GOOD SAMARITAN LAW

From time to time there are celebrity overdoses that are plastered all over the news. River Phoenix (1993), Chris Farley (1997), Anna Nicole Smith (2007), Heath Ledger (2008), Michael Jackson (2009), to name but a few. What was going on in the general population was equally horrendous. The CDC would later report that opioid deaths decreased the life expectancy of the entire population of the United States. NCHS Data Brief No. 328, November 2018.

In 2011, New York passed its 911 Good Samaritan Law. This statute "allows people to call 911 without fear of arrest if they are having a drug or alcohol overdose that requires emergency medical care or if they witness someone overdosing." NYSDOH Fact Sheet, 3/16.

So, make sure you know which law might cover you, in which situation, and which won't.

DRAM SHOP ACTS

These laws have a funny name. Back in the 1700's, in England (where this law originally comes from) if you went into a bar and ordered gin, they would ask you, "How many drams do you want?" The liquor was sold by drams, small teaspoonfuls, that held about 3/4 of today's size teaspoons.

Because of this practice, bars and pubs began to be nicknamed "dram shops." Eventually, the name stuck to an entire set of laws that only apply to bars and restaurants that serve alcohol.

The dram shop acts intersect with tort law when it comes to serving intoxicated people. These laws are popular around the country. New York's law is representative. Section 11-101 of the New York General Obligations Law makes it illegal to serve alcohol to any customer who is "visibly intoxicated." Things like red eyes, falling asleep at the bar (it happens), staggering, and slurred speech are all signs of intoxication that employees are supposed to be trained to spot. Once an employee observes that conduct, no more alcohol is to be sold to that patron.

Further, anyone injured by a drunk customer who was served alcohol can sue the customer, the bar and the individual bartender who served that customer.

One might think that, after an accident, finding evidence that an establishment served a drunk would be hard to come by, but you'd be mistaken. These cases are common. Your author was deeply involved in a Bronx Supreme Court case that started in 2004. A drunk driver killed a worker at a Bronx construction site. The family sued the driver, who was now in jail, the City of New York, and the MTA, for failing to provide her husband with a safe place to work. After years of investigation and discovery in the lawsuit, eyewitnesses turned up who allegedly saw the intoxicated driver being served at my client's seedy City Island bar, just before the accident. Sure enough, in 2009, my client was impleaded into the lawsuit.

As it turned out, by this time, my client was embroiled in his own complex set of unrelated business lawsuits and had no insurance for the claim, and no attachable assets. After the defendants found that out, the case was eventually settled, and my client escaped liability. He died in 2015.

HOW NOT TO USE THIS BOOK

We need to pause here and relate a brief tale about a former student who demonstrated that a little knowledge is a dangerous thing. Your author places this story here as it indirectly relates, as you will see, to the dram shop acts.

I had a nice student a few years ago. Nicole was about 35, reserved in class, and smart. A year after she took my course, and graduated, she contacted me for my (free) opinion about what had happened to her.

She went out with a girlfriend on a Saturday night. They were both from the Bronx. She took an Uber car. Her girlfriend was driving her own car. They met up in the suburbs, north of New York City, and went to a bar. Nicole said she was "already wasted" from drinking at a prior bar. Lesson number one: do not get drunk in public.

As her friend was served drink after drink at this second bar, Nicole was still drunk, but she was no longer drinking alcohol. The place was packed and busy. The male bartender suddenly said to Nicole's friend, "How are you getting home? Are you driving?" The friend insisted she was fine, and was served another drink. A little while later, another bartender served the friend still another round. My former student, for some reason, now begins to remember the dram shop acts from her business law class. As she was turning these ideas over in her mind, the first bartender came back. He said directly to Nicole, rather aggressively: "How is your friend getting home? Is she okay? Do you know how she's getting home? You have to call a cab!"

At this point the whole situation could have probably been defused, but here, Nicole made a second error, and said, rather loudly and sharply, perhaps slurring a word or two, "Why do you keep serving her? You're violating the dram shop act! That's a violation! You're violating the law!" That was the wrong time to bring up an obscure legal doctrine with an overwrought bartender.

The bartender immediately snapped his fingers and gestured toward a female manager and a big male bouncer, and said angrily to both women, "You're out of here! Both of you! Pay your check and get out!" Instantly the manager, and the burly employee, were next to them. Nicole drunkenly thinks to herself, "This is a bad situation. I better call the cops!"

This is another mistake people sometimes make with the law. They perceive a situation backward, often due to drink or drugs, and call the police on themselves. Sure enough, in about 10 minutes, two uniform police officers strolled casually in the door to the crowded bar. To get their attention, Nicole stood up, smiled and waved at them, as if they were delivering pizza. It probably looked to them like she was not taking the situation seriously from the get-go.

After they got her side of the story, she heard one of the cops address the bartender by his first name. That was when she knew she was in trouble. Sure enough, the bartender, and the young cops, seemed to be old pals. The bartender said the two females had been told to leave but refused (not exactly true). Nicole and her friend were told to stand up and turn around. They were handcuffed, and arrested, on the spot, for criminal trespass and disorderly conduct.

It turned into a miserable experience. She didn't get out of whatever jail they took her to for hours. Of course, the charges were later postponed and, when she did not get into any more trouble, they were dismissed.

The moral of the story is do not flaunt your knowledge of the law, especially in the wrong situation. It can get you in trouble.

THE FIREMAN'S RULE

People do not realize that they can be sued by a fireman, or a policeman, as they come charging through the house trying to keep everyone safe. Interestingly, you can't be sued if the firefighter gets injured by the fire, nor if the policeman is injured by the criminal he or she is chasing. But you can, and will be sued, if the fireman falls through your cellar steps because the stairs were falling apart. You can also be sued if the policeman falls over your kid's roller skates that were left in a walkway.

Hence, the name "The Fireman's Rule." Your narrator had one case of this kind, when a first responder was injured in a fall onto glass, on my client's vacant Bronx lot. We claimed that the 1935 New York's Fireman's Rule (General Municipal Law § 205-a) did not apply to vacant lots. The case eventually settled for a reasonable amount.

These cases are reported in the media from time to time. The contractor overseeing the Deutsche Bank demolition work, in Manhattan, after the World Trade Center disaster, settled with the families of two firemen killed in a 2007 fire. In 2014 a firefighter sued a Staten Island homeowner, alleging a shoulder injury. Macy's was sued by a firefighter, and his wife, when he slipped on garbage, while reporting to a fire at the Staten Island Mall, in May of 2016. Shapiro and Annese. "Firefighter Sues Macy's." *N.Y. Daily News*, 16 Sept., 2018, p. 88.

LOSS OF SERVICES

Notice that a spouse may also sue, in a personal injury case, where there has been "a loss of the other spouse's services," due to the injuries suffered in the accident. Services include housework, cooking, companionship and sex.

DANGER INVITES RESCUE

This is fairly rare doctrine in American tort law. But, like an odd relative, it has its place. Modern life is wonderfully safe. But stuff does happen. And it happens suddenly, and devastatingly. Trains still crash, and escalators still malfunction.

This doctrine comes into play when there is an accident, resulting in a suddenly dangerous situation. It tries to protect, and encourage, people who are heroes and help in emergency situations, if they can. As long as the hero does not cause the accident in any way, if they are injured, they can sue along with anyone else hurt.

The defendant will not be allowed to claim, at trial, that the hero has no standing because they were injured while sticking their nose where it didn't belong. Nor can they claim that the injured hero "assumed the risk," nor that he or she was guilty of contributory negligence. The legal reasoning is that the "danger" that the defendant put the plaintiff in, actually "invited" the injured person to go and perform a "rescue." Hence: danger invites rescue.

An injured hero can lose a case like this. The defendant may prove the innocent person was not really in danger, or that the hero's reaction was not reasonable. However, the doctrine has been successfully applied, in Illinois, to people who were injured preventing a suicide *Strickland v. Kotecki*, 234 Ill.2d 553 (2009). It was also used in a Connecticut case where a mother was hit and killed by a train because she was running to rescue her young child, who was too close to the track, *Cote v. Palmer*, 127 Conn. 321 (1940).

SOCIAL HOST LIABILITY

This is a new, and fast changing, area of the law. Social host laws have caught many a homeowner by surprise, and they can result in huge legal problems for anyone hosting a party with a lot of drunk, or drugged, guests. The laws impose both criminal and civil penalties that come into play when a drunk guest crashes a vehicle, or gets into an altercation. It doesn't matter too much if the injuries to the plaintiff occur at the party, or shortly afterward on a distant roadway. The host can be held liable.

These laws are closely related to the dram shop acts, because they can place liability on those who serve others alcohol or drugs. In the 1980's, spurred by consumer safety groups, social host laws, with varying degrees of severity, were enthusiastically passed around the United States.

The problem is keeping up with these laws in each state. In New York and California, the focus is on underage drinking. So, in those states, if a person under 21 is hurt or hurts someone else, after drinking at your party, even though it was a private party, you can be sued as the social host. If everyone is over 21, you're off the hook, at the time of this writing (2020). But, again, the legal trend is toward more liability for private party hosts.

As an attorney, your author was sometimes asked advice, by friends in trouble. One such incident demonstrated how insidious social host liability can be. My friend, Nora, who lived in another state, flew out west for a three day business conference. A few days after she came home, I received a breathless call from her. She was in pieces. "I got arrested when I got off the plane." I couldn't believe it.

It turned out her teenage son had held a huge party for many of his underage, local school pals, while she was away. It got out of hand. News of the party spread, and dozens of kids showed up. A lot of alcohol was served. One of the young partygoers was killed in a car accident after the party. Nora's picture, doing the "perp walk" for the cameras, in handcuffs, was in all the papers. She began a three year journey into a legal nightmare. She eventually got off with a fine and a long probationary period.

PREMISES LIABILITY (AS A RESULT OF OWNING LAND)

In English law, the concept of owning and profiting from land, began and ended with the king. The reigning king and queen owned everything, and all titles, leases, permits and other uses of land flowed from them. As the system relaxed, property ownership of the rich was recognized, but the rights and responsibilities, first set in law in feudal times, continued.

So the liability for owning land went through some contortions. At first there was no liability at all. If you fell and broke your wrist on your lord's property, you'd do well to keep it to yourself. Gradually, the law began to change. The difficulty was this key issue: what duty did an owner owe to the various people who came on his or her land without their knowledge or consent? Eventually a three part system was developed. (1) No duty was owed to trespassers. If they got hurt, too bad. (2) Some duty was owed to a "licensee," like a salesman, who came on your property to sell you something. (3) The highest duty was owed an invitee, someone who you somehow actually invited onto your property.

As you can imagine, all those issues generated constant, complex legal litigation with endless arguments about what category the plaintiff was in, who invited them where, etc.

For the U.S., California finally ended it, in the 1960's. California changed its laws, ruling that a landowner just needs to use ordinary care to protect anyone on the land from any reasonably foreseeable hazards. The property can be a condo, a farm, a residential house, it does not matter. That California law caught on around the country. That's why, today, a landowner can be sued by a trespasser who falls down an unguarded well.

PLANES, TRAINS, BUSES AND HOTELS

Certain businesses owe more of a duty to the general public than others. The reason is because these businesses take almost total control of you, when you use their services. 'Think about it. You get on a plane, or a train, or stay in a hotel. You probably have no idea how to operate the systems in the jet, locomotive or the building. You are unaware of what the risks are in that industry. Yet, you're okay with being sealed in there with everybody else, exposing yourself to possible contagious viruses, accidents, food poisoning or a host of other crazy stuff that has already actually happened to other people just like you.

So, cruise ships, airlines, bus lines, and railroads are called "common carriers" because they commonly (meaning every day) carry stuff (passengers and freight). They owe their customers a "duty of care" also sometimes called a duty of "utmost care." Hotels are covered by similar "innkeepers laws."

It seems prudent to be aware of this. Such businesses have more of a duty toward you and your company. And, if you are in one of those businesses, then you, in turn, owe a higher duty of care to your patrons.

DEFENSES AGAINST NEGLIGENCE

Defendants in negligence lawsuits, like any action, are free to claim a lack of jurisdiction, or a lack of standing on the part of the plaintiff, or the statute of limitations has run out, or that the venue is wrong, and must be moved.

The defense will also usually try to attack each element of the negligence tort. If the defense can knock out any one element (O.U.C.H.: duty, breach, cause, injury) then the plaintiff, and their attorney, will both be thrown out of court.

Therefore, defendants will often claim, through their lawyers, that they had no duty to the plaintiff. Or that the duty was met, and any injury was sustained elsewhere (no breach of a duty). Intervening and superceding causes are popular "causation" defenses that attack the element of proximate cause.

The defendant can also make a counterclaim against the plaintiff, claiming the plaintiff owes him money, or injured the defendant in the same occurrence. If there are co-defendants in the action, a cross claim will be made blaming the co-defendant for the situation. Defense counsel may implead (sue) other parties and bring them into the action, as "third party defendants." They will be accused of being the ones who are actually responsible for the plaintiff's injuries.

Once the technicalities are disposed of and the elements are established, the defenses against negligence really boil down to only two.

The first is contributory negligence. This is when the defendant claims that the plaintiff caused their own injury, through their own carelessness, and the defendant owes them nothing.

Down through the years this rather harsh rule has changed slightly and nowadays we have, in most states, some form of comparative negligence. In these states, the jury finds the relative percentages of fault, for all the parties in the lawsuit. The total must equal 100%. The percentages in the verdict are then applied to the money amount(s) that the jury determined. In the *Liebeck* case, with the spilled coffee, the percentage of the plaintiff's comparative negligence was deducted from the total dollar amount of her jury award. The verdict amounts are then written down in a judgment, to be filed in the county clerk's office.

The other defense is assumption of risk, although this is rare. It almost always applies to activities like sports, such as skiing or basketball. Normally, you cannot sue if you are injured while playing these sports, because you "assumed the risk" that you might be hurt. Even if an injury is caused by a foul, in a game like basketball, that is considered part of the game and any resulting lawsuit will be dismissed.

There are still successful negligence cases brought against schools and parks, where the assumption of risk defense can be dismissed. But, in those cases, the plaintiff can usually prove that a dangerous hazard existed on the field, that could have been corrected. A sharp fence where baseball is played, or hidden holes in a football field, would yield a premises liability case. In those circumstances, assumption of risk would either be defeated as a defense, or would be ruled inapplicable.

DAMAGES DEFENSES

Students of business law sometimes have a misunderstanding about a liability defense versus a damages defense.

In America, auto passengers are required to use seat belts in vehicles equipped with them. In a case where a passenger does not wear a seat belt, and is injured in an accident, the opposing attorneys will sometimes claim the lack of a seat belt as comparative negligence. That is incorrect. The lack of a seat belt does not cause a crash. A passenger is rarely guilty of any comparative negligence in a motor vehicle case unless they cover the driver's eyes or do something equally as stupid. Lack of a seat belt is a defense in "mitigation of damages." What that means is, at the trial, the defendant's lawyer can put in evidence about the issue and then request, on summation, that the jury award less money, in terms of the damages, because of the lack of a seat belt.

THE BIFURCATED TRIAL AND THE STRATEGIES THAT GO WITH IT

Most civil trials today are bifurcated. There are some exceptions. Bifurcation means that the liability, or fault, portion of the trial is completed first. Then, if the defendant is not liable, the whole case is over, and everyone can go home.

But, if the defendant is found to be liable, then the judge (in a non-jury case), or the judge and jury, hear more evidence and deliberate until the amount(s) of money damages that the defendant will pay is finally decided.

In this bifurcated situation, each team of lawyers will have a specific set of strategies and goals, as to how the two part case will be won or lost. Plaintiff's counsel wants to get 100% liability against the defendant(s), or else, get the highest percentage possible. Then, they want to score big money in the damages phase of the trial. A high percentage of liability multiplied by a large damage award equals a large total monetary verdict. Often, in negligence cases, the plaintiff's attorneys will lend the client the money for the case expenses. At the end of the case, they get that expense money back, and then they take one third (1/3) of the entire recovery, as their fee.

But their adversaries, the defense team, wants to prove 100% non-liability, or, at least, get a verdict with the lowest percentage of fault against their particular defendant. Then they want to hold the damages to a minimum. A small percentage of liability multiplied by a small award equals a small total verdict. The defendant's attorneys are usually paid by the hour while all this is going on, and the hours add up fast on a trial.

The judge is in the middle, trying to push the trial to its conclusion, without making a major legal mistake. Any serious error will result in a mistrial, or a verdict that has to be thrown out, or, worse, a verdict that is later reversed by a higher court, and then sent back for a retrial. There have been cases where attorneys were fined, because they intentionally caused a mistrial when they realized they were going to lose.

7. BUSINESS TORTS

There are certain torts that are uniquely committed by businesses, so these are categorized as such. One of the key federal statutes in this area is the Lanham Act of 1947. It governs trademarks and unfair competition and repeatedly surfaces in advertising and misrepresentation cases.

OPERATING WITHOUT A LICENSE

Certain businesses and professions require a license from the city, county, state or federal government. If such an entity causes another firm to incur losses, whether through neglect or intentional conduct, a good plaintiff's lawyer will investigate whether the defendant was properly licensed or not.

The reason is that, when drafting the plaintiff's complaint, one of the separate claims that can be made is unlicensed operation. The plaintiff may lose on the other counts in the complaint, but can still salvage a win with unlicensed operation.

Typical companies and professions that need licenses are nail salons, taxis, lawyers and doctors. Once in awhile an unlicensed operation case is picked up by the media. In 2018 a Croton-on -Hudson, New York man was arrested for making an unauthorized radio transmission. His pirate station was broadcasting on 98.5 FM. He called his show, "La Mojada." Hudson Valley Post, Dec., 2013.

PALMING OFF

It still happens. Someone buys a Rolex watch, cheap, near Times Square in New York City. When they get home they realize they bought a Rodex watch. But the d was covered by the minute hand when the customer was first shown the timepiece.

This is an example of palming off. In England it's called "passing off," which sounds less dignified. It is selling a product that is somehow misrepresented as someone else's. Cases like this often come under a general rubric of unfair competition.

There's even something called reverse palming off, which is slightly different. Whereas regular palming off is usually done by being clever and sneaky, reverse palming off is where one company removes a product's original trademark and then somehow manages to sell the goods under a completely different name.

PRODUCT DISPARAGEMENT

Why aren't there more commercials that prove, with facts, side by side, which is the better product? Why aren't car commercials more factual instead of stating "best in class" or "selected by" some magazine?

The reason is the tort of product disparagement. If a company is caught making an untrue factual statement in an ad about a competitor's product, they are going to get sued. And they are going to lose. So they try to be careful, and advertise with what is called "puff."

Puffing or puffery is making claims such as a product is "the best of all" or "far and away better than all of the competition." It is completely legal. Why? Because those statements are opinions. No business person is expected to say their product is mediocre. So, an exception is made in this area, and a business is allowed to make biased, "exaggerated claims," as long as they are presented in the form of general opinions, rather than actual established facts.

FALSE ADVERTISING

Much of the general public misunderstands this tort. Many people believe that if a news ad has a misprint that says "TV's are on sale for $1," they can run down to the store and force them to sell a TV for $1. 'Not so.

An ad in a newspaper is not a formal offer to enter a contract of sale with the reader. That printed ad is legally considered an offer for you to come into the store to make a legitimate offer. You may know that you can walk into almost any store in America, see a price tag, and offer a salesperson to buy it for less money. Sometimes you can get a "floor model" at a discount. An older model can sometimes be purchased for less that the "sticker price." So the prices in American stores are fluid, and can change daily, for any number of reasons. Therefore, a misprint, especially when the fault of a third party, like a separate printing company, does not normally bind the company selling the goods.

What false advertising really is, is repeated fake sales, bait and switch games, and falsely advertised lower prices. A rogue company can unfairly destroy competitors with lies, usually over a substantial period of time. Not only can other businesses that are injured sue and collect money damages, they can also theoretically get an injunction. An injunction is a strict court order prohibiting a business from engaging in specific conduct. An injunction can apply presently, and for the future.

But, in the real world, people and companies often don't have the resources to fight false advertising tactics, so they just go out of business. The Crazy Eddie case, in the 1980's, is an egregious example of false advertising and fraud. The electronics chain put dozens of competitors out of business, as it grew to over 40 stores and raked in hundreds of millions of dollars. Then it collapsed under a mountain of lies and fake accounting.

CIVIL FRAUD

At the outset, let's remove an area of confusion. This section deals with the tort of fraud. This kind of fraud occurs between people involved in business, and results in a lawsuit. In some states it is known as intentional misrepresentation. The crime of fraud is a different animal and will be dealt with later.

Someone commits civil fraud when they (1) knowingly (2) lie about an important fact in their business dealings and then (3) a victim innocently relies on that misrepresentation, and (4) the victim ends up losing money.

This is another tort whose main elements can be remembered with a simple spelling aid which can help some people: F.A.K.E. contains the elements of civil fraud: F, for false fact, A for Acted upon by the victim (relied on), K for Knowledge - the defendant knew he or she told a lie, and E for Expense (loss) to the victim.

At an actual trial of a case like this, the attorneys will battle over side issues that prove, or disprove, the main case. How important was the lie? Did the victim know more than she claims? Was it reasonable for the victim to rely on the information received?

A well known case in this area is *Parrott v. Carr Chevrolet, Inc.*, 17 P.3d 473 (2001). In this case a man bought a 1983 Chevvy Suburban truck, and got a Frankenstein vehicle in return for his hard earned money. The Vehicle Identification Number (VIN) was missing from the door. The odometer appeared to have been tampered with. There were no emission controls on the engine. The defendant told the buyer a lot of work had been done on the truck and they would correct any problems. Conflicting statements were in the truck's "Special Disclaimers and Conditions" papers compared to the defendant's "Buyer's Order." In the end, the vehicle the plaintiff had been sold was so totally illegal, his insurance company refused to insure it. It was literally useless as a vehicle to be used on public roads in Oregon.

As is typical with these things, the plaintiff complained and the defendant did nothing. So the plaintiff complained louder, and there were some half hearted attempts to satisfy the customer. Finally there was an argument of some kind, and both parties stomped off, upset.

Except Mark Parrot sued and won. He not only won, but he was awarded punitive damages. It is very rare in civil cases, but punitive damages are sometimes permitted in very serious cases. The jury is allowed to make an award to, literally, punish the defendant, and to make them an example, so that others will be deterred from similar conduct. Mr. Parrot was awarded $11,496.00 in compensatory damages and $1 million in punitive damages.

The trial judge then intervened and reduced the punitive damages to $50,000.00. The plaintiff's attorneys were allowed to request an award of attorneys fees (rare) from the judge, but the court only awarded them $15,000.00 out of their claimed $55,468.75 bill.

Both parties appealed and the next highest court, the Court of Appeals, reinstated the $55,468.75 lawyer's bill. The case was then appealed again and went all the way up to the Supreme Court of Oregon. That final court reinstated the $1 million punitive damage award, and let stand the higher attorney's fee. A total win for the plaintiff, demonstrating civil fraud and punitive damages.

INTENTIONAL INTERFERENCE WITH CONTRACT

This business tort is often threatened, but rarely sued upon. It tries to prevent someone with a contract from breaking the agreement because a better offer has come along. The elements are straightforward. The defendant (1) knows of a contract someone has with a third party. The defendant (2) intentionally (3) induces the third party to breach that contract with the plaintiff, thereby (4) damaging plaintiff's business.

These cases arise in the sports world when one agent steals a player from another, or a team tries to steal a star player from their rivals. It also arises, in conjunction with non-compete agreements and non-disclosure agreements, when key executives or scientists jump from one company to another.

BREACH OF THE IMPLIED COVENANT OF GOOD FAITH

This is another changeable area of the law. While all states have some kind of implied expectation of honesty between people in a contract, there can be some disagreement as to whether there is a separate legal claim for such a breach. Sometimes, it comes down to individual judges. Some might dismiss such claims, as being included in any run-of-the-mill breach of contract allegation.

In your narrator's career, this "bad faith" claim was used mainly against insurance companies and other instances where the the nature of the contract was very personal, and required the parties to totally trust each other. Anyone who has ever been involved in an insurance claim knows how different buying and using insurance is, from, say, buying and using a computer, or food.

Illustrative of the principle is *Gourley v State Farm*, 3 Cal. Rptr. 2d 666 (1991). Ms. Julie Gourley was a passenger injured in a car accident. She was not wearing a seat belt. The collision was caused by an uninsured drunk. She made a claim under her own insurance policy for accidents with uninsured drivers. Her insurance company's employee lied to her and told her that her lack of a seat belt was the legal cause of her injuries. They wanted her to take $20,000.00. She eventually went to arbitration and was awarded $88,137.00. She was so upset with her treatment, she sued State Farm for breach of the implied covenant of good faith and won. She was also awarded $1,576,000.00 in punitive damages. The court felt that State Farm had dealt with her in a dishonest, hostile way, although it was being paid insurance premiums to protect her.

STRICT LIABILITY

There are some cases in America where the defendant is found responsible for damages quickly, in a cut and dried manner, without any evidence of fault, or lack of care. These cases are called "strict liability" cases. They cover activities that have repeatedly been shown to be so risky, and difficult to control, that complete safety can never be totally guaranteed.

Businesses with operations that are abnormally dangerous are, therefore, subject to these claims. Companies that perform crop dusting, blasting, or make fireworks, and people who keep wild animals on their property, all can be held strictly liable for any damages that result to others.

This is why, if blasting will take place at a site near yours, someone will come around with a camera, first, and photograph your property thoroughly. That's to protect the company from any false claims of blast damage that was pre-existing.

All a plaintiff needs to do in these cases is to prove the defendant was engaged in the activity, and that the activity caused the injury. No proof of fault, nor precisely how the defendant made a mistake, is required.

PRODUCTS LIABILITY

Most of the power tools, cars and appliances we buy on a daily basis in our country are safe and dependable, labor saving devices. But, when one of these modern machines has a hidden defect, or does not come with proper labels and warnings, it can severely injure its users. That's why, when you buy a ladder, today, there are safety stickers all over it.

Products liability claims do not apply to the services provided by a firm. It is manufacturing companies that worry about this modern tort, and most manufacturers are exposed to this liability on a continuing basis, while their product is in circulation.

This type of legal claim began in California, in the 1960's, and grew out of the laws originally passed to ensure clean and wholesome food products for the general public.

The complaint in a lawsuit of this nature may also contain claims of negligence, misrepresentation and fraud. The plaintiff's team will be trying to put in evidence to win on one, of more, of these separate theories, along with the products claim.

The elements for products liability cases goes like this: If the the jury finds that (1) the end user of a product was injured, (2) while using the product in a way in which it was intended, and (3) her or his injury was the result of a defect in the design and/or manufacture, of which (4) she or he was not aware and (5) which made the product unsafe for its intended use, then the verdict will be for the plaintiff.

In the elements mentioned about, a breach of a duty of care is not mentioned. Since the liability is "strict," there's no deduction for the plaintiff's negligence. Also consider that, even if a user modifies the product slightly, takes a safety guard off, or uses it in an unapproved manner, or it's used by someone without any prior experience, the manufacturer will still be held liable. Usually it's because the product maker can be shown to be aware of customers making such modifications, and using the product in unorthodox ways. To be free of liability the maker must prove that the plaintiff completely "misused" the product, or assumed a risk that was open and obvious to anyone with common sense. Punitive damages are very rare, but can be claimed if the defendant company was reckless in its actions.

By the 1970's, in the United States, these product liability laws had become so troublesome in some industries, that manufacturing ceased. One example was general aviation. Manufacturers of small planes began going out of business in the 1980's. Some were buried under lawsuits for old planes manufactured years before. Thousands of jobs were lost as the industry fell apart.

Something had to be done, and the lobbyists descended upon Washington D.C. Public interest groups faced off against the manufacturing companies. Years of wrangling resulted in the General Aviation Revitalization Act of 1994. This law protects manufacturers of small aircraft from liability for accidents involving planes that are more than 17 years old, at the time of the accident. Oddly, this concept is not a statute of limitations, because it does not run from the date of an accident. It is a "statute of repose," because any claims repose (go to sleep) at the specific deadline, which runs from an event that did not involve harm to the plaintiff.

8. NEW LAWS

At this point, let us take a breather in our strenuous studies of settled law, and take time to consider how different jurisdictions wrestle with the issues of today, on a daily basis. The northeastern states have been in the forefront of legal experimentation for the last few decades of American life. If there's a big legal ruling in the northeast, it's a good bet that similar law will be spreading soon, across the U.S.A. Here is a review of just a few of the new laws that the modern manager should be ready for.

THE SEXUAL HARASSMENT REFORM BILL

New York State enacted a new sexual harassment law. It extended the statute of limitations, with regard to sexual harassment claims, from twelve months, up to three years. Plaintiffs also no longer have to prove harassment was "severe and pervasive" in order to win their case. The new law also requires that any nondisclosure agreements between companies and victims must include wording that clearly preserves the victim's right to sue any responsible party. Shahrigian, Shant. "Sex Harass Bill Signed." *N.Y. Daily News*, 13 Aug., 2019.

IDENTITY THEFT AND LARCENY CAN BE DOMESTIC VIOLENCE

In 2019, New York's Governor, Andrew Cuomo, signed a package of bills into law that broadened the definition of what is considered "domestic violence" under state law. Coercion, identity theft and larceny can now all be considered domestic violence. So that victims can escape their abusers, the new laws also allow a victim to report crimes anywhere in the state, rather than just where they took place. Slattery, Denis. "New Protections For Domestic Abuse Victims." *N.Y. Daily News*, 9 Aug., 2019, p. 120.

A COMPLEX MINIMUM WAGE LAW

The minimum wage is always a hot button of controversy. Recently, New York revamped some of its old minimum wage laws. Because of different categories of workers, and different regions, the resulting minimum wage scheme is a little more complex than you might think. Just check out this quote, direct from the labor.ny.gov website: "In New York City [the minimum wage] is now $15.00 per hour for all size businesses. In Nassau, Suffolk and Westchester counties, it is $13.00 per hour. In the remainder of the state, it is $11.80 per hour. There are different hourly rates for workers in the fast food industry and those who receive tips."

So, three categories of workers, in three regions. It probably should be called the Minimum Here-and-There Law.

THE ERIC GARNER ANTI-CHOKEHOLD ACT

This new statute was passed in Albany, and signed into law in 2020. It is named after Staten Island resident, Eric Garner, who was choked to death by a New York City police officer, in 2014. The law adds a new section to the New York Penal Law §121.13. Although chokeholds were already banned by the New York City Police Department, this law defines them as the crime of aggravated strangulation, and makes them a class C felony. Madubuko, Allison and Sneed. *New York State Police and Criminal Justice Reforms.* Volume X, Number 196. Natl L. Rev. (2020).

AN EXTENDED STATUTE OF LIMITATIONS FOR RAPE SURVIVORS

As a result of the nationwide #MeToo movement, in 2019, modifications were made to the Criminal Procedure Law in New York State, extending the statute of limitations for second degree rape to 20 years, and for third degree rape to 10 years. N.Y. Crim. Proc. Law § 30.10.

The statute of limitations for a second degree criminal sex act and for second degree incest were also increased. Shahrigian, Shant. "Rape Laws Get Tougher." *N.Y. Daily News*, 19 Sept., 2019, p. 2.

STYROFOAM IS BANNED

New York City banned Styrofoam on January 1, 2019. Under this law, commercial food establishments may not offer, sell or even possess, what are called "single-use foam food containers." Also no one can sell, nor offer for sale, those annoying loose little foam packaging thingies (called "packing peanuts").

The New York Department of Sanitation will issue you a written violation that carries a $250.00 fine if you're guilty under this ordinance. For a second offense, you'll pay $500.00, and thereafter $1,000.00 for each offense.

There are exceptions for raw meat, eggs and fish. Also, pre-packaged food, that is sealed prior to delivery to the customer, can still use Styrofoam.

As often happens, N.Y. State then got on the bandwagon and banned "expanded polystyrene (EPS) foam products." New York joined Maine, Vermont, and Maryland with this ban. The full effect of the state ban commences in January of 2022.

CHANGING STATIONS

In 2018, New York City mandated baby changing stations in new or substantially renovated buildings. New York State copied it a year later. All bathrooms used by the public must have a changing table, and a sign indicating where it is.

GENDER ON A BIRTH CERTIFICATE

New York City passed a new law that allows city residents to choose a gender-neutral marker, "X," on their birth certificates. There is no longer any need to provide a letter from a doctor, or an affidavit from a health care provider, to change a person's gender. Jorgensen, Jillian. "Birth Certs Will Have 'X'.", *N.Y. Daily News*, 10 Oct., 2018.

BIAS AS TO HAIRSTYLES AND CLOTHING

In 2019, New York State amended its Human Rights Law, and joined California to become the second state in America to ban discrimination based on a person's natural or cultural hairstyle. Styles like braids, twists and dreadlocks are now legally protected.

Assemblywoman Tremaine Wright (D-Brooklyn) said we needed to end the "problematic practice of hair discrimination." Slattery, Denis. "Law Bans Bias." *N.Y. Daily News*, 13 July, 2019.

The Religious Garb Bill prohibits discrimination, in all of New York State, on the basis of religious attire and facial hair. So turbans, yarmulkes and hijabs are okay, when worn on the job in N.Y., unless they present some kind of safety hazard. Slattery, Denis. "Battle vs. Bigots." *N.Y. Daily News*, 10 Aug., 2019, p. 17.

IT IS ILLEGAL TO ASK ABOUT A CRIMINAL RECORD BEFORE MAKING A JOB OFFER

A 2015 law makes it illegal, in New York City, to ask a job candidate about their criminal record until after a job offer has been made. That little box that is on every job application form you have ever seen that says: "Check here if you have ever been convicted of a crime," is banned in the five boroughs. Whether it really disappears from every form used in the city remains to be seen. People have a way of slipping into bad old habits if a change in the law isn't vigorously enforced. Spina, John. "'Don't Ask' Law." *N.Y. Daily News*, 20 June, 2015.

IN NYC, IT IS ILLEGAL TO ASK WHAT AN APPLICANT WAS MAKING

This is another new, progressive law. In order to eliminate gender wage discrimination, the City of New York outlawed the usual practice of asking a job candidate what they made at their prior job. This was first tried with city agencies, but was eventually expanded to all employers. Jorgensen, Jillian. "Illegal To Ask Salary History." *N.Y. Daily News*, 5 May, 2017.

HUMAN RIGHTS LAWS EXTENDED TO INDEPENDENT CONTRACTORS

Effective February 8, 2020, the anti-discrimination rules in the New York State Human Rights Law (NYSHRL) which originally only protected employees, are now applicable to contractors, subcontractors, and other "gig workers." So an independent contractor may now bring a claim of workplace discrimination, harassment, and/or retaliation under the NYSHRL.

Like the above changes to New York State law, New York City also amended the New York City Human Rights Law (NYCHRL) to make clear that independent contractors are entitled to the same anti-discrimination protections as traditional employees.

THE UNEMPLOYED ARE A "PROTECTED GROUP"

The New York City Council overrode then Mayor Bloomberg's veto, in 2013, to pass this local law. It makes it illegal for businesses, with four or more employees, to discriminate on the basis of a person being unemployed. The law creates a new private claim for unemployment discrimination in the advertisement and hiring process. Victims are allowed to sue alleged violators for damages. Raphan, Eric, *Unemployed Are Now Protected*, Labor Employment Law Blog, April 10, 2013, www.laboremploymentlawblog.com.

DOG WALKING, AS A JOB, IS ILLEGAL WITHOUT A LICENSE IN NYC

New York City Health Department rules ban anyone from accepting money to care for an animal outside of a licensed kennel. You cannot board, feed or groom an animal, for a fee, without such a kennel license. All those people you see walking dogs in Manhattan are probably violating these regulations. On the other hand, many people feel such rules are old hat and need to be changed. Durkin, Erin. "Hounding Sitters." *N.Y. Daily News*, 20 July, 2017, p. 20.

REMEMBER THAT SOME PEOPLE IN NY HAVE DIPLOMATIC IMMUNITY

While this is not a New York law, it is certainly a New York "situation." Because Manhattan is home to the United Nations, every once in awhile New Yorkers get a reminder of an odd legal concept called "diplomatic

immunity." This is a well known idea, between nations, going back many years. To allow diplomats to operate freely in foreign countries, and to avoid false charges being brought against them for political purposes, diplomats are given immunity from prosecution from certain laws and taxes where they work.

For instance, in 2017, a Sudanese diplomat groped a woman at a bar in the East Village, and the police caught him, but they had to let him go. The victim told the police that Hassan Salih grabbed her breasts and buttocks, at 2:30 in the morning, near Third Avenue and 13th Street. The cops chased the perp, and cuffed him. But he later proved that he was, indeed, a diplomat, and he was released. Dimon, Laura. "Diplomatic Immunity In Grope." *N.Y. Daily News*, 10 Oct., 2017.

YOU CAN'T PERFORM AN ACT WITH ELEPHANTS IN NEW YORK STATE

In 2017, New York passed the Elephant Protection Act. It outlawed the use of pachyderms in any entertainment acts, including circuses, carnivals and parades.

FROM JERSEY, MASSACHUSETTS AND PHILLY: OKAY TO USE CASH

This is an odd law that came from other jurisdictions, but you may soon see similar statutes put forth, or railed against, as time goes by. New York is considering the need for such a statute.

More and more firms are insisting that their customers pay them with a credit card or other method, regardless of what the patron may desire. New Jersey Governor Phil Murphy signed a law making it illegal to refuse to accept cash at any New Jersey business. Massachusetts enacted a similar law 'way back in 1978 and Philadelphia banned cashless eateries in March of 2019.

DISCRIMINATION ON THE BASIS OF WEIGHT?

An assemblywoman from Manhattan has proposed legislation that would outlaw discriminating against a person on the basis of their weight. Her measure would also outlaw any discrimination in hotels, restaurants or other public places.

Democrat Linda Rosenthal introduced the bill in Albany in 2017. "Weight discrimination is seemingly one of the last acceptable forms of discrimination," she said. Blain, Glenn. "But Weight!." *N.Y. Daily News*, 27 Sept., 2017, p. 19

9. BUSINESS CRIMES

Just as there is a class of private wrongs that are business torts, there is a class of crimes that are business crimes. In this chapter we will look at business crimes in general, and, specifically, what pitfalls they hold for people and companies.

WHAT'S A CRIME?

This question goes back to the earliest days of the human species. It is a fine, broad subject for philosophers. We look at the definition in 21st century, legal terminology. In the U.S., a crime is a public wrong (as opposed to a tort, which is a private wrong). It is an offense that is in violation of a person's obligation to other people, and to the state, and for which there is a high probability of punishment. A crime is thought of as injuring us all, as collective members of the society. Very often, a tort and a crime are committed together, at the same time. If a criminal defendant has assets or applicable insurance coverage, they will often be civilly sued by their victim(s), while their criminal case is still pending.

KINDS OF INTENT

The leaders of our country have tried, not always successfully, to make sure that only guilty people are punished by our penal system. Therefore, a defendant's good or bad intent emerges as a crucial issue, in each accusation. Intent can often be inferred by the facts and circumstances that surround the events in question. What was said? What was done?

For our purposes, we will not study intent as deeply as a second-year law student might. There are four main levels of intent that intertwine with business crimes and torts.

First, there is a complete lack of intent, also known as negligence or carelessness. This almost never exposes a defendant to criminal liability. However, if the negligent conduct is so gross that it rises to recklessness, usually defined as a disregard for human life, then one can be arrested for negligent homicide or criminally negligent manslaughter. That total recklessness can be thought of as the second kind of intent.

Next up the ladder is general intent. This is when someone is driving a vehicle or working with a dangerous tool. They generally intend to move the vehicle forward or do the work they are doing. That kind of general intent is enough to convict someone if they violate a stop sign ordinance, or some safety regulation. This is why you cannot get out of a ticket for passing a stop sign, in traffic court, by saying, "Sorry, Judge, I just didn't see it." You just admitted that you are totally guilty.

The highest level of intent is specific intent. This is the kind needed to convict someone of a serious crime. Specific criminal intent is when someone takes some action with the knowledge that they are doing something legally and/or morally wrong, for a selfish purpose. If you rob a bank with a threatening note, you are aware, as you walk in, that the money you will take out is not yours. But you still intend to take it. That is your specific intent. Now, if you are doing this as a bank employee, to test security, and the money goes back to the bank, then what you are doing is legal. There's no criminal intent. But, if the reason you are taking the money is to keep the cash for yourself, and buy things with it, while avoiding capture, you have crossed over into criminal intent.

ELEMENTS

There are only two elements to a crime: (1) criminal intent (see above) and (2) some criminal act. That is, some action or conduct that is in furtherance of the criminal intent. If the intent to is to steal, sneaking into the premises at night is the criminal act. If the intent is to harm someone, the act is punching them.

CLASSIFICATIONS

The traditional breakdown of crimes is misdemeanors, for lesser crimes, and felonies, for the most serious ones. Although the distinction is starting to blur in some jurisdictions, felonies are usually punishable by more than one year in jail. You may sometimes read about a defendant being sentenced to one year, plus one day, in jail. That means it was a felony case and the court felt a felony sentence was warranted. Violations, on the other hand, are small offenses, usually punishable by a fine.

CRIMINAL PROCEDURES THAT DIFFER FROM CIVIL SUITS

Because of the differences between torts and crimes, the procedure in how the cases are started and handled is slightly different.

A criminal case begins with an arrest. There are two kinds of arrest, with a warrant or without.

ARRESTS AND WARRANTS

An arrest pursuant to a warrant is demonstrated by the classic undercover narcotics sting. If the police find out, from an anonymous tip, that hard drugs are being sold from a specific location, they will send in an undercover officer to try to make a "buy." Once a purchase is made, the undercover will log the drug evidence into the police property room, and then write out an affidavit stating who was involved and what happened. The prosecutor will then write out an application (a motion) to the local judge, asking for an arrest warrant to be issued for the person, or persons, selling the drugs. Since some drugs can be quickly flushed down a toilet, the prosecutor often asks that the warrant be a "no knock" warrant, allowing the police to break in suddenly, and quickly grab the evidence. Such procedures are so dangerous and controversial that some jurisdictions have outlawed such warrants.

The prosecutor will annex the undercover's affidavit, and any other evidence available, to his or her papers, to convince the judge that the arrest is legitimate. Once the judge signs the warrant, depending on the circumstances, the police either politely knock on the door, during business hours, or they arrive at 4:00 a.m., and break the door down with a battering ram.

When the police see a crime being committed, or when there is probable cause that a felony was committed, then people can be arrested without a warrant.

SEARCH INCIDENT TO ARREST

Once an arrest is made, whether pursuant to a warrant or not, the police are allowed to search the person arrested, and the immediate surrounding area (i.e., for instance, a car nearby), for weapons or evidence. This is called a search incident to arrest. It's based on the theory that officers have to be allowed to eliminate the possibility that a suspect could suddenly grab a nearby gun or knife, which has happened in the past.

GOING THROUGH THE COURTS

After the shock of the arrest, a criminal case wends its way through the courts the same as a civil case, just with less paperwork. Prosecutors can bring a case to trial by themselves, with an "information," or by convening a grand jury and having them indict the defendant. Grand juries usually consist of between 16 and 23 people and they meet for 18 months at a time, handling case after case. If the grand jury returns a verdict of a "True bill" in an action, then that means the grand jury felt that there was sufficient evidence of a crime to put the defendant on trial.

The defendant is then arraigned. The arraignment is a proceeding in which the court tells the defendant what charges are being made against them, and takes the defendant's plea. The pleas can be guilty, not guilty, or nolo contendere. Nolo contendere means the defendant is not admitting guilt, but he or she will not contest the charges against them. Defendants will often do this when they know they are going to be sued by their victim. A guilty plea can be used against them in the civil suit, but the nolo plea cannot.

The parties then engage in some limited discovery and the case is set down for trial. Usually, but not always, these criminal proceedings go much faster than a civil case. Before the trial there are usually court conferences in which the controversial concept of plea bargaining enters the picture. The two sides see if a deal can possibly be worked out. Witnesses and evidence are used like bargaining chips to induce the defendant to plead guilty or to get the prosecutor to make a better offer. The district attorney does not want to lose a trial, but the defendant docs not want to take the chance of getting a long prison sentence. Hence, the majority of cases are pleaded out.

The two favorite pleas amongst the author's criminal defense colleagues are the A.C.D. and the reduction to a lesser charge. A.C.D. stands for "adjourned in contemplation of a dismissal." It postpones the criminal case indefinitely, but if the defendant is not re-arrested in six months, the case is dismissed. The reduction to a lesser charge is where a defense attorney can get an accusation reduced from a felony to a misdemeanor or from a misdemeanor to a violation.

If there is no plea, the case goes to trial with a judge or a judge and jury. At this point, the parties are starting to lose control of the situation. The more evidence that goes before the finder of fact, the harder it gets to settle the case amicably. Anything can happen. There could be a mistrial. There can be a plea in the middle of the trial. Once the case goes to verdict, neither party can control what happens and the court and jury determines the winner and the loser. Following post-verdict motions, the only thing left in a case is the appeal, if the defendant is convicted.

MONEY LAUNDERING

Your author was in a seedy after-hours club in New Jersey late one Saturday night in the 1990's. The place was empty, so I remarked to the sole bartender, "It's a dead night tonight."

He leaned forward, smiled, and said, quietly, "Oh no. I see lots of people on the dance floor. This place is packed tonight!" I was taken aback. He said that he knew for a fact that the bar owners were reporting record crowds, and huge profits, every Saturday night. As we continued talking, I began to feel foolish. I had not recognized an obvious money laundering scheme. To this day I have no idea why he divulged that. I never went back, and never saw him again.

It goes like this. Someone sold a lot of drugs, or stolen goods, or embezzled a lot of money. They have a lot of stolen cash in their physical possession. They got away with their crime, so far, but they must keep a low profile, say, in a suburban neighborhood. Although they could afford one, they cannot suddenly start driving a Rolls Royce around town. So, how do they enjoy the fruits of their criminal labor? They launder their illegal money. By creating false records, they can "wash" the money, create a legal trail for it, then spend it legally without arousing suspicion.

Usually, they create a fake business, or a real one that operates fraudulently. Then they funnel their stolen money through the business, in the form of imaginary "profits." They may even hire a legitimate accountant, report the profits, and pay the taxes on them. Then they deposit what is left into their bank account, like any other solid citizen. After a few years, the last act in the drama unfolds. They indicate less profits for the fake company and close it down. Bars and restaurants are great for this type of thing because there's lots of crazy, fake expenses to claim, it's a high cash business, people can skim some cash off the top, and, after some time, nobody really knows how much cash was made, who was there, nor how much money anyone spent.

THEFT

Theft covers a whole range of offenses. Robbery and burglary are separate crimes, but they are both forms of theft.

In most states the crime of theft is broken down into petty theft, and grand theft. New York uses the term "larceny." Stealing something worth less than $1,000.00 in the Empire State is petit larceny, a class A misdemeanor. (N.Y. Penal Law § 155.25.) If the stolen goods are worth more than $1,000.00, then it's grand larceny in the fourth degree, a class E felony. (N.Y. Penal Law § 155.30.) In California petty theft is stealing something worth less than $950.00. So different states have slightly different applicable amounts and names.

A fairly odd case in California demonstrates how the felonies and misdemeanors interact in a real scenario. A man named Paul Gonzales was accused of luring women to expensive restaurants, ordering the most expensive food and wine items on the menu, then quietly leaving, and abandoning the victims with the check. Because he did this many times, he was charged with felony extortion, and attempted extortion, and his bail was set at $350,000.00 on those serious charges. Eventually, based on what the prosecutor could prove, L.A. County Judge Darrell Mavis upheld only two misdemeanor charges against the defendant. They were defrauding an innkeeper (leaving without paying), and petty theft. Bail was reduced to $100,000.00 on those less serious accusations. Dillon, Nancy. "No Felony Charges." *N.Y. Daily News*, 21 Sept., 2018. Mr. Gonzales eventually pleaded no contest and was sentenced to 120 days in jail and three years of probation. He was also banned from going on the dating websites, PlentyOfFish and Bumble.

BURGLARY

Burglary was , traditionally, entering a dwelling at night with criminal intent. The specifics of this crime could be important, back in the day. That was because, in most jurisdictions, the commission of a burglary allowed a dwelling owner to use of immediate deadly force to kill the intruder, to prevent a felony in progress. Of course, a civilian is not covered by any immunity, as a policeman might be, so the premises owner had to be right. If the intruder turned out to be a relative that forgot their key, the homeowner was in deep legal trouble.

ROBBERY

This crime is the taking of property by force, or the threat of force. The typical city mugging is a robbery. Using a gun to rob a convenience store is a robbery. There are differing degrees, depending on whether the defendant used a weapon or used the assistance of an accomplice. In most states robbery statutes are serious felonies that carry prison terms of three and a half years and up.

RECEIVING STOLEN PROPERTY

On the street, someone who receives stolen property is called a "fence." They are as important to a burglary ring as the burglars are. Without this criminal's financial and marketing connections, burglars cannot sell anything. A lot of pawn shops, knowingly or not, run afoul of this law. Also, every once in awhile, a pharmacy, or bar, gets caught.

There are only two elements to this offense, but they can be a challenge to prove. (1) The defendant must know the goods they are receiving are stolen. This is inferred from the circumstances by law enforcement, because no one ever says, nice and loud, "Thanks for the stolen goods!" (2) There must be specific intent to keep the goods, or sell them, thereby denying the real owner's rights.

ARSON AND INSURANCE FRAUD

Historically, arson was the burning of a dwelling. Over the years, partly because so many homeless people sleep in cars, it now covers setting fire to anything that belongs to someone else. This crime runs hand in hand with insurance fraud.

A business will get into financial trouble but be covered by a policy of fire insurance. The temptation is always there to set a fire and collect the insurance cash. There are clues when this is going to happen: Financial problems, the inability to pay for proper maintenance on a building and failing on monetary obligations.

WHITE COLLAR CRIMES

More money has been stolen, through what are known as white collar crimes, than any other way. According to the FBI, such crimes cost the U.S. about $300 billion a year. In contrast, three or four thousand bank robbers only steal an average of $10,000.00 per robbery, every 12 months. That is a paltry $35 million a year.

The term, "white collar crime," was coined around 1939 and there is still some disagreement as to what, exactly, constitutes white collar crime. White Collar Crime, Cornell Law School, Legal Information Institute, www.law.cornell.edu.

The FBI has defined it as "those illegal acts which are characterized by deceit, concealment, or violation of trust and which are not dependent upon the application or threat of physical force or violence." Barnett, Cynthia, The Measurement of White Collar Crime, Dept. of Justice NIBRS Series, undated pamphlet. Since extortion can carry the threat of violence, some people do not classify it as a white collar crime, while others do.

Also, the reader may note that some of the offenses in this section seem entwined with each other, or with other crimes entirely. That is not incorrect.

As we try to categorize this type of human conduct, the crimes will often overlap and interrelate.

FORGERY

Forgery is creating a fake document, or modifying a real one, to gain something. It could be money, an object, legal power, or an advantage over someone. The key issue is, did the forged document somehow change the rights and liabilities between the parties to the document? Of course, creating a fake check, or increasing the amount on a real one, will cause money to be taken out of the account, without the owner's consent. So that forgery slightly changes the rights and liabilities of that account holder.

People who routinely use the boss' signature stamp, and the spouse who routinely signs the other spouse's name to a weekly paycheck, both have permission to do so, and lack criminal intent. Therefore, they are not committing forgery, although it looks like they are.

Forgery is mainly a state crime, coming under the police power. Identity theft, which we will discuss soon, is also a type of forgery and is a felony under federal law. Counterfeiting money and forging federal documents such as immigration documents, licenses or military certificates, are also federal crimes.

EXTORTION

Extortion is the legal term for what we all call blackmail. Companies are facing more and more of this type of crime, some of it perhaps state sponsored. There must be some threatened force or fear involved to be extortion. "If you don't pay me $100.00 a month, I will publish embarrassing pictures of you," is extortion. So is this: "If you don't pay me $100.00 a month, I will punch you in the face." There may never be any real pictures, nor a punch thrown. It is the fear that is the heart of the matter. And the actual threat can come from many different directions.

Hackers holding a company's computer system hostage with "ransomware" is a form of blackmail. Corporations, school districts, and even government entities have fallen prey to the sophisticated hackers operating today.

THE COMPUTER FRAUD AND ABUSE ACT

To try to combat these developments, the federal government enacted the Computer Fraud and Abuse Act (a/k/a the CFAA). It was originally passed in 1986. It has been repeatedly amended, most recently in 2015. It outlaws accessing computers without authorization, and using a computer to commit fraud, extortion or the stealing of data, money or passwords. 18 U.S.C. § 1030. The law also creates a private right to sue, allowing anyone damaged by a violation of this law to obtain compensation from the violator and/or injunctive relief.

Sadly, it seems that the government is two steps behind the computer criminals, and the CFAA has been roundly criticized as outdated. Gabriel Ramsey, an attorney in San Francisco has said that "Legislators need to work from the ground up with an overhaul of this statute." Bannister, Adam, US Computer Fraud and Abuse Act, Portswigger Web Security, 14 May, 2020, portswigger.net.

CRIMES INVOLVING CREDIT CARDS

There is a trend in the Unites States to make crimes involving a credit card a separate offense.

States deal with this issue in different ways. New York has passed statutes forbidding credit card use for fraud, or for using an outdated or revoked card. But mainly, the usual host of laws against larceny and fraud are utilized. Texas has written a section into their penal code that covers credit card crimes. Texas Penal Code § 32.31. California also has a section of their penal code devoted to "access cards," as they call them. Offenses are punishable by up to a year in jail, depending on what was stolen or damaged. California Penal Code §§ 484-502.9 et. seq. (Credit Card Fraud Laws).

The federal government incorporated credit card laws in its U.S. Code, providing a $10,000.00 fine and a jail term of 10 years for the use of a fraudulently obtained or stolen credit card in interstate commerce 15 U.S.C. § 1644.

Of course, the statutes above would always be charged in addition to basic criminal charges of fraud and larceny.

Usually, the person who had their credit card stolen, or hacked, is not liable for the charges. That is because they did not make the card, nor create the elaborate security system that is supposed to protect against fraud. That is all the bank's doing – to protect their investment. However, if someone acts really stupid, and it can be proven that they were extremely careless with their card, then the credit card company can dispute their obligation to reimburse the account.

CAN YOUR CHECKING ACCOUNT GET YOU IN TROUBLE?

The answer is yes. The most likely scenario for trouble with your account is writing a check for which you have insufficient funds. Depending on how that goes down, you could be in for a world of hurt. Most of the time, the check recipient notifies you, and you replace the check with another, or some cash. However, if you are already involved in a dispute about a payment for car repairs, and you pay with a rubber check that bounces sky high, the vendor may go right to the police.

The key in these cases is knowledge. Did the check writer know that there was not enough money in the account at the time the check was written? People do this all the time, and then deposit enough money to cover the check, just before it gets to their bank. When you do this, be aware that you are playing things close to the edge, and if your plans get screwed up, you may get a call from a detective rather than a creditor.

CHECK KITING

The other way checks are used in business crimes is a practice called kiting and is a constant concern for the banking industry. Kiting is where a perpetrator moves checks between accounts with false names, taking advantage of the slight delay between a check's arrival somewhere, and the actual receipt of the cash it represents. Through repeated skillful manipulation, an astute criminal can temporarily inflate the balance in an account, with those fake checks. Then a withdrawal is made, of real money, and the criminal disappears behind the pseudonym used. Soon, the bank realizes the criminal's deposited checks were all bogus, and they are missing some money. More advanced computers and faster systems make this crime more difficult by the day, but criminals are resourceful, and it still happens.

EMBEZZLEMENT

This is a statutory crime, based on a written law. It is the stealing of property that someone has entrusted to the defendant. Businesses are continually victimized by this crime. Executives entrusted with huge amounts of money, to get large, complex projects completed, are always tempted to create a fake company and start approving real payments for fake services. Anyone high up on the corporate ladder would have the knowledge, and the ability, to create the necessary paperwork to cover up such a scheme.

Your narrator often tested classes with a final exam which contained a fact pattern in which a fictitious school administrator would embezzle the funds of the college they were working for. Then, in 2017, we were a little surprised to see that a former administrator for the City University of New York was arrested. He allegedly pocketed thousands of dollars based on fake accounts. Carmine Marino, 43, was accused of stealing money from 2007 to 2012, while he was the budget and finance director of CUNY's School of Professional Services. Bekiempis, Victoria. "CUNY Worker Is Busted." *N.Y. Daily News*, 8 Apr., 2018.

CRIMINAL FRAUD

In the chapter on business torts, we studied civil fraud. This section is about the crime of fraud. Certainly, the elements are similar and the crime and tort can be committed simultaneously.

Criminal fraud is obtaining property by deceiving someone. Normally, these crimes are more involved than merely selling a truck that cannot be insured, as in our civil fraud example. In these cases, a defendant is selling a building they do not own, or is involved in a phony stock scam.

MAIL AND WIRE FRAUD

Anyone who saw the 1993 movie The Firm, starring Tom Cruise, may recall that, at the end of the film, Cruise's character realizes that every fake bill that had been sent out by the criminal law firm was a separate count of mail fraud. That is what eventually cracks the case and delivers justice to the villains, in this classic thriller from director Sydney Pollack.

Mail and wire fraud are federal crimes. They are committed any time a person mails or electronically transmits material in furtherance of a dishonest plan.

These crimes are used in employment fraud, lottery fraud, telemarketing schemes and sweepstakes cons. The list is endless, and every year the scammers think of a few more good ones. Almost no one in America is immune. Older people are especially vulnerable as they sadly fall prey to all sorts of con games, Ponzi schemes, "boiler rooms," and pump and dump operations. While some progress has been made, the problem is a frustratingly stubborn one. Be on the lookout for this in your business and personal life.

IDENTITY FRAUD

According to a study from the Javelin Strategy & Research, a fintech consulting firm,14.4 million Americans were victims of identity fraud in 2018. This is a huge area of business crime today. The government is trying to stamp this out, but it is like a game of whack-a-mole.

The Identity Theft and Assumption Deterrence Act of 1998 makes identity theft a federal crime punishable by a large fine and a prison sentence of several years, depending on the circumstances. It also enlists the aid of the Federal Trade Commission (the FTC) to act as the federal government's front line in the effort against identity theft.

The states have their own identity theft laws. New York's Penal Law § 190 covers identity theft, with a range of offenses, from a misdemeanor, to a class D felony.

As a business manager the key is being super careful with customers' and company data, having a top notch IT department, hopefully with the latest software, keeping viruses and hackers out of your system, and having a well-trained, sharp-eyed staff.

BRIBERY

This ancient crime has one very odd characteristic that sets it apart from almost all of the crimes we study. This crime requires at least two people, but they are not a perpetrator and a victim. Instead, as in a conspiracy, they are both guilty.

Bribery is when one person gives something of value to another person, to gain an unfair advantage over other competitors. And yet, such conduct is not always a crime in some cultural settings. As soon as you go offshore, the legal picture changes drastically. These problems show the thorny issues western democracies face as they deal with increasing global trade in the next few decades.

The result, in the U.S., was the Foreign Corrupt Practices Act of 1977. It outlaws bribing foreign officials and people running for office in other nations. So the exchange of very expensive gifts, to celebrate business agreements, is still done, legally, in certain countries.

THE RICO STATUTE

Most people in America have heard of the RICO Statute at some point, or other. The initials stand for Racketeer Influenced and Corrupt Organizations Act, a federal law passed in 1980. 18 U.S.C. § 1961.

A racketeer is someone who engages in crime in an organized, consistent, professional way. An impulsive cat burglar, who works alone, is not a racketeer, but a mafia captain is. Several states have enacted their own state RICO laws, patterned after the national one.

The law was first used against traditional organized crime gangs (the "corrupt organizations"), but recently has broadened out and been used against the Hells Angels (acquitted), the Latin Kings (pending), and FIFA, the international soccer club organization (several guilty pleas).

To get a RICO conviction, a prosecutor must prove the defendant was part of a group that benefitted from a pattern of racketeering activity. That "pattern of racketeering activity" is, in turn, proven by showing that the defendant committed, or was involved in committing, two felonies, within

10 years. The felonies that come under the RICO umbrella read like a bad list of career choices: gambling offenses, murder, kidnapping, extortion, arson, robbery, bribery, counterfeiting, securities fraud, money laundering, embezzlement and terrorism.

The interesting thing about RICO is the punishment. When found guilty, the defendant must pay a $25,000 fine, and do up to 20 years in prison for each separate racketeering incident (i.e., for each "count" of the criminal complaint they were found guilty on). But the thing that makes the news is that the defendant forfeits every possession, each bank account, asset, boat, car, airplane, jewel, and house that was bought with racketeering money. This has left many a defendant and their family broke after conviction, rendering expensive legal appeals difficult.

Missing from the RICO list is dealing in illegal narcotics. Drug trafficking is now largely prosecuted under a different federal law, called The Kingpin Statute. The full name is the Continuing Criminal Enterprise Statute. 21 U.S.C. § 848. Like RICO, it requires proof of a series of felony drug violations. A guilty verdict results in a mandatory minimum twenty years' imprisonment, with a maximum of life, plus, a fine of up to $2 million, and forfeiture of all the profits in the criminal drug enterprise.

The key takeaway here is, hopefully you will never even hear of a prosecution under these powerful laws, but in any case, know two things: (1) The prosecutor has to prove a pattern of crime. And, (2) if anyone is guilty, they are going to lose all their stuff.

INCHOATE CRIMES

Inchoate crimes are serious transgressions that get a person into deep trouble, although, in the end, a planned crime may, or may not have, been committed.

There are three types of these. They are (1) attempted crimes, (2) conspiracy and (3) solicitation.

ATTEMPTED CRIMES

Logically, if a person tries to commit a murder, but only succeeds in injuring someone, they will be charged with attempted murder. The same goes for a whole host of crimes across the criminal spectrum. "Attempted" can be attached to almost anything. So there's attempted murder, attempted robbery, etc.

CONSPIRACY

A conspiracy is when (1) two or more people agree to commit a crime, and then (2) take some step, even a small one, toward committing it. Once those two events occur, the parties are guilty of conspiracy to commit that crime. It does not matter if their attempt is later abandoned, nor if it fails.

Consider this example. Two students are upset with their law professor. They agree to wait by the road, after class, and capture him. One student buys rope, and another puts a bat in her car. They are now guilty of a conspiracy to kidnap. If they go to their chosen ambush spot, but their teacher goes home a different way, they are still guilty.

If a crime does occur, however, defendants who act together can be charged with both the main crime, and for the criminal conspiracy to commit it.

SOLICITATION

Solicitation traditionally starts with someone sidling up to someone else and furtively whispering, "Psssst. You wanna make some money?" Of course, what follows is a scheme to make some cash with a dicey plan where somebody ends up missing some funds. If that happens to you, you are being solicited to commit a crime and the other person is guilty of criminal solicitation.

AIDING AND ABETTING

When a person assists another in the commission of a crime, or in avoiding capture, that is considered aiding and abetting. In New York, it is called hindering prosecution and a first offense is a class D felony. NY Penal L §

205.65 (2012). This applies to people who hide criminals, support them somehow or give them some assistance.

The reader may recall a case that rocked America for weeks in the spring of 2020. George Floyd, a 46 year old black man, was killed on May 25, while in custody of the Minneapolis Police Department. Four policemen were fired, and then arrested. One officer was charged with murder. The other three were charged with aiding and abetting. It emerged, early on, that the Minneapolis Police Department, like many others, had a specific rule, sometimes called a "duty to intervene policy." Police officers are required to step in, and stop colleagues from using excessive force. Condon and Richmond. "Twin Cities Pioneer Press." twincities.com, 7 June, 2020. Like many such regulations, for various reasons, it is an easy thing to write, but a very difficult duty to abide by and enforce.

OBSTRUCTION OF JUSTICE

This is an offense having broad application. It can encompass perjury but is usually used when people resist arrest or interfere with the arrest of another. In New York it is a class A misdemeanor, called obstruction of governmental administration, and it includes preventing a public servant from performing their official function. It also outlaws interfering with emergency services by radio, telephone or television. NY Penal L § 195.05.

An example of how these charges are applied was illustrated after a fatal accident, in Brooklyn, in 2019. Right after the May 27, 2019 wreck, that killed a motorcyclist, Jasmin Morales-Cruz, of Queens, confessed to driving the 2014 Infiniti involved in the accident. She was allegedly going 80 mph, while she was drunk. But the police were suspicious. So, they retrieved video from bars, interviewed witnesses and got the text messages from that night, between the car's passengers. The texts showed they all agreed to lie about who was driving the car. Morales-Cruz was charged with obstruction of governmental administration and hindering prosecution. McShane, Larry. "A Carful of Lies." *N.Y. Daily News*, 4 Sept., 2019, p. 5.

Another situation that this charge can involve is when people film the police. As long as you stand back, don't interfere, in the vast majority of cases, you are allowed to video the police in action. However, there are circumstances where this can be a sticky situation. California, for instance, has very strict laws about filming people and consent. Also, sometimes, a situation gets out of control and the police will overreact and you might get arrested anyway.

A Queens man, Ruben An, 26, was recording the New York City police speaking to a homeless man on a Manhattan street. Officers asked him to step away and avoid blocking the sidewalk. He was arrested for obstruction of governmental administration. A jury acquitted him. He sued the City, claiming a deprivation of his First Amendment rights. He reached an amicable settlement without a finding of fault. Greene, Leonard. "He Settles Case of Filming." *N.Y. Daily News*, 12 Oct., 2018, p. 26.

CORPORATE CRIMINAL LIABILITY

Can a corporation be found guilty of a crime by a jury in America?

Undoubtedly, yes! A corporation is considered a legal entity, like a person is. It's considered an imaginary legal thing that has rights and liabilities, and a duty not to act in a criminal way.

Now, you might wonder, can a corporation be put in jail? No. But it can be fined. Plus, anyone who committed crimes on behalf of the company, such as executives and employees, can be sent to prison.

Some very famous companies have committed crimes, at various times in their existence. BP pled guilty to felony manslaughter, environmental crimes and obstruction of Congress and paid a record $4 billion in criminal fines and penalties for its conduct leading to the 2010 Deepwater Horizon disaster. U.S. Dept. of Justice. (2012, November 15). BP Exploration and Production Inc. Agrees to Plead Guilty. [Press release].

Also convicted at one time or another: British Airways (price fixing), HSBC (money laundering), Korean Airlines (price fixing), Pacific Gas & Electric (causing a wildfire), Sears (credit card fraud), Volkswagen (cheating on emissions), Carnival Corp. (dumping oily waste, then violating probation), Takata (faulty airbags), Olympus Medical (failure to file infection reports), ZTE (sending tech to Iran), to name but a few.

10. CONSTITUTIONAL PROTECTION

Most modern governments have tremendous, far reaching power over their populations. When someone asks why Americans have so many strong rights, an apt answer is that, when we are accused of a federal crime, the complaint is entitled the "United States of America versus." Since there are about 330 million Americans, the government has a huge advantage, in terms of money and resources, when it comes to convicting any one defendant. That's why we need strong rights, which stem from the federal Constitution.

FIRST AND 14th AMENDMENTS

It might seem odd, for the First Amendment to land here, in a section of this book following crimes. But, think about it, when someone is arrested for loitering, what about the right to assemble? Free speech? Also, such statutes are notoriously vague. Can one really tell what is outlawed by reading the statute? The 14th Amendment (1868) made all federal rights and privileges involved in these issues equally applicable to the states.

A case in point. Birmingham, Alabama. It's 1962. The defendant was found guilty of violating a city ordinance that stated: "It shall be unlawful for any person or any number of persons to so stand, loiter or walk upon any street or sidewalk in the city as to obstruct free passage over, on or along said street or sidewalk. It shall also be unlawful for any person to stand or loiter upon any street or sidewalk of the city after having been requested by any police officer to move on.'" The U.S. Supreme Court felt the statute was vague. It made a police officer the ultimate judge of who can remain, and who must leave, the sidewalk. That interferes with First Amendment liberties, and sounds a lot like life in a dictatorship. The defendant's conviction was reversed. *Shuttlesworth v. City of Birmingham*, 382 U.S. 87 (1965).

117

SECOND AMENDMENT

The Second Amendment, standing for the right to keep and bear arms, is sometimes involved in weapons possession cases. The debate on this issue has been raging for decades and opens new wounds every time there is a controversial shooting in the U.S. and the world.

The key recent case in this area was the landmark case of *District of Columbia v. Heller*, 554 U.S. 570 (2008), the U.S. Supreme Court upheld the individual's right to have a firearm within the home, for self-defense. Membership in a state militia is irrelevant.

FOURTH AMENDMENT

The Fourth Amendment is a powerful weapon against the illegal search and seizure of things by the federal and state governments. It covers everything: real estate, possessions, papers, computer files, and personal items. The government must obtain a search warrant, by convincing a judge that the police are being reasonable in the scope, timing and reasons for the piercing of the Fourth Amendment protections.

Searches without a warrant are only legal when a perpetrator is trying to destroy evidence, or as part of an arrest (see the chapter on Business Crimes) or after evidence of a crime is seen, right in plain sight.

If a search is improper, any items seized will not be permitted in evidence at any resulting trial. This is the controversial "exclusionary rule" (because it "excludes" evidence), and has roots going back to the 1700's. Sometimes, an entire criminal prosecution will fall apart because of this rule. For example, in a drug case, if all the drugs and records that police seized in the defendant's house can't be admitted into evidence, there is no case left to prosecute. What the defendant was selling, and how he or she was running their drug business, cannot be shown to the jury.

Business premises are no different than a residence. A warrant to search is usually necessary. However, employees must always remember that their computer belongs to the company. With just a few words, a manager or business owner can consent to an employee's computer and records being

118

seized, searched or copied. If consent is granted by the business, there is no need to obtain a warrant, and any evidence found in that workplace, as long as it is material and relevant, will be admissible at any subsequent trial.

THE FIFTH AMENDMENT

Ah, yes, the Fifth Amendment. Everyone has heard of this. There are jokes and stories about it. But it is real, and can have real repercussions for you, and for your business.

James Madison came up with this one, in a speech he gave in the brand new House of Representatives. The actual paragraph has several parts to it. The initial section deals with the need for grand juries to indict people for very serious crimes. The second section establishes that a person cannot be tried twice for the same crime, commonly known as double jeopardy. Next, the amendment states that a defendant cannot be compelled to testify in a criminal case. Lastly, it states that there must be due process of law (i.e., a trial) before the government can throw someone in jail, and the government must pay compensation if it has to take someone's property for a new road, or park, or something.

The basics of the words are easy to understand, but there are some twists and turns to this fundamental law. We will take this one section at a time. The part about the grand jury is of more interest to local district attorneys than business. But the next section, dealing with double jeopardy, is important to everyone.

DOUBLE JEOPARDY

The Fifth Amendment only forbids trying a defendant a second time for the exact same crime, for the exact same conduct. So, if A kills B, and A is later acquitted of both murder and manslaughter, he cannot be tried again, for the murder or manslaughter of B. Depending on the statute of limitations, A can still be charged with other crimes involving B, and his family. A just can't be tried again for the murder or manslaughter of B.

This is why lawyers laugh when they watch a movie like the Paramount Pictures' Double Jeopardy (1999). The film has been roundly criticized, and rightly so, for completely misconstruing the Fifth Amendment. Worse, the filmmakers amateurishly overlooked the fact that district attorneys are notoriously clever at working the system against the accused. In serious cases, defendants can usually be re-arrested, and tried, for a whole host of additional charges, if necessary.

Some critics feel that this right concerning double jeopardy has been under attack for some time. Others say that's a good thing, because this right has been used to circumvent justice. In the 1950's, the southern United States was a civil rights battleground. Reformers in the federal government had known for some time that, although laws were in place that were supposed to apply to everyone, certain popular criminals could never be convicted in any resulting jury trials. Once they were acquitted, the federal government could not try them again, because of the Fifth Amendment. However, there was an old law called Title 18, with a chapter, from 1940, dealing with how it's a federal crime to deprive someone of their civil rights. The government in Washington, D.C. began using this obscure law to prosecute people who got away with murder with friendly juries. Title 18, U.S.C., § 242.

Soon, well known defendants, who had beaten state murder charges, found themselves on trial on separate federal charges for depriving their victims of their civil rights. The courts upheld the procedure on the grounds that murdering someone deprived them of all their rights, forever. Plus, such a criminal charge was not a prosecution for the exact same crime. In 1968, they amended the statute and added that a person could be sentenced to life in prison, if the deprivation of civil rights resulted in a death.

TESTIFYING AGAINST YOURSELF

The next section of the Fifth Amendment deals with self-incrimination. This right goes deeply back into the past, including England, but it never seemed to really be applied as it is in America today. What surprises most people who come into contact with this concept is how limited it is in the modern world.

A criminal defendant can be required to participate in a lineup. They can be required to say the same words the perpetrator said out loud during the crime. If the defendant refuses, or uses a funny voice to avoid detection, there can be unfavorable testimony about that at the trial. The court can compel the defendant to supply hair samples, blood samples, and other bodily fluids.

Note that we are taking about a defendant who has been arrested. We are not talking about a suspect who has not been accused of a specific crime yet. The district attorney can apply to the court for an order to get samples from a defendant who has been charged with a crime. A court order for a mere suspect, who has not been charged with any crime, is much harder to get. In those cases, the police will usually observe the suspect, and try to grab a cigarette butt, or coffee cup, anything the person put their lips to, and then threw away. They will get their DNA sample that way.

So, if the Fifth Amendment prevents testimony against yourself, how come you can be compelled to provide all this stuff, which will probably convict you, if you are guilty? That's because the courts have narrowly, and controversially, interpreted this right to apply solely to oral, or written evidence. So the police, or D.A., can't make you write out your version of what happened. They can't force you to answer their questions about a crime, nor make you take the stand, at your own trial, to force you to testify as to what happened.

If the police do ask someone a question, and they answer it, that can be used against them. Here, the Fifth Amendment bumps up against the "Miranda warnings." *Miranda v. Arizona*, 384 U.S. 436 (1966). The legal theory is a suspect should know his or her rights before they waive them. Hence, the warnings of the right to remain silent, and the right to a free lawyer.

TAXES

But, what about taxes? Isn't that written testimony sent to the government, which can then be used to convict you?

The current legal thinking on this, is no. Not everyone is convinced. Here is the logic. The reader can then make up their own mind.

Filing your taxes is different, in a few ways, from being accused of a crime. These differences allow the government to compel you to file a tax return, if you make $12,200.00 or more.

The Fifth Amendment differs from filing taxes because the amendment only applies to people accused of wrongdoing. The statement you make to the Internal Revenue Service is not about wrongdoing. It stems from one's relationship to the government, not because one is accused of a crime. Providing income data is different than providing evidence because it is universal. Everyone who makes over a minimum amount of money has to file a return. And, all you really must do to comply with the law is file, report your income and pay any taxes you owe. The IRS will even happily figure your taxes for you. ('Don't let them.) The final result is different, too. In criminal proceeding there can be a formal trial, and an acquittal, or a fine, or jail, and the Fifth Amendment relates to it all. In tax filings, your information just results in you paying "your fair share," as they say.

JUST COMPENSATION AND EMINENT DOMAIN

At the end of the Fifth Amendment is this section. Certainly, if your business has to be moved through "eminent domain," the taking of private property for a public purpose, there will be compensation. However, as we saw in 2020, this does not apply to a government ordered shutdown, to stop the spread of a virus. In that case, financial bailout programs are the only recourse, because the government is not taking private property to use it for its own purposes. It is inadvertently damaging businesses to stop a pandemic.

LEGAL IMMUNITY

Immunity must be discussed here, as it dovetails with the Fifth Amendment. One would think that immunity would be a good thing to be given, right? Yet, many a person given the privilege of immunity found themselves between a rock and a hard place. It has long been known as a "tool" for prosecutors.

There are different ways immunity can be offered or granted. Sometimes, if a witness stands on their Fifth Amendment right to not answer a question, a judge can grant immunity "on the record," at a trial or hearing. The witness must then answer, or risk being held in contempt. Or it can be more complicated. Immunity can be contained in an actual written statement, or a contract, given to a witness or to a defendant, or their attorney, in court.

Once immunity is granted, if a person is charged with the underlying crime anyway, the defendant actually pleads immunity, as a defense. In that respect, immunity can also be waived, but that is rarely done. Receiving a get-out-of-jail card, which immunity can sometimes be, is very hard to release. But some crucial witnesses, in major cases, have received immunity and gotten out of jail, only to be publicly assassinated a few days later.

PRIVILEGES

Certain human relationships are recognized throughout the law. Marriage, adoption, partnerships, and professions, all have separate, dedicated laws applicable to them and their businesses. Spouses are entitled to bring loss of service claims if their mate is injured. A parent can sue for the loss of services of their child.

The closest of human relationships result in specific, recognized, legal "privileges" that prevent certain people from being questioned about a defendant. The most well known one is the attorney-client privilege. A lawyer cannot be legally compelled, by court order, subpoena, nor any other method, to divulge information about a client. The client may waive the privilege. The attorney may not. Even after a client dies, information is not to be revealed unless it is necessary to carry out the client's estate wishes.

Other established privileges are the spousal privilege (a/k/a/ the marriage privilege), which applies both to communications between the mates, as well as preventing each of them testifying against the other. The privilege grows out of the ancient idea that, for legal purposes, a married couple were considered one person. This privilege must be suspended in divorce proceedings, child custody disputes and especially in domestic abuse cases.

Other privileges are the psychiatrist-patient, priest-penitent (or, pastor or rabbi) and parent-child. A few states recognize an accountant-client privilege, but not many. New York does not. Neither does New Jersey.

11. CONTRACTS

Our entire planet runs on the simple concept of "the agreement." This thing, where two sides agree to exchange one thing for another, is how we run our lives, how we feed our families, and how we strive for some enjoyment in our existence. Your grocery store, the cable TV company, your Internet service provider: they all provide these goods and services to you, based on contracts.

WHAT IS A CONTRACT?

A contract is a legally binding agreement. In other words, it is an arrangement of sorts. The agreement sets out what each party is obligated to do, and when. What elevates something to a contract is that the entire arrangement can be enforced by a court of law. That is because evidence can be produced, orally or with reliable documents, that can clearly demonstrate to a court the intent of the parties.

So, a contract is a legally enforceable oral or written agreement, that, if breached, can be sued upon in court, to obtain relief.

ELEMENTS OF A CONTRACT

Your author's law firm handled many real estate closings and business deals. The first thing we always did was to acco the important contracts into a file folder with those metal prong fasteners, so prevalent in offices all over America. That term eventually provided a handy mnemonic to remember the elements of a contract.

Since, you ACCO a contract into a folder, remember that A is for Agreement. The contract must contain some kind of arrangement. The courts sometimes use the term "a meeting of the minds." There should be some type of offer and an acceptance, or a promise in return for money, or services. But the parties' agreement, duties and obligations should be clear. They will control any resulting litigation.

The first C in ACCO stands for Consideration. A court will always look to see if both sides put something into the contract. It can be money, or work or materials. But, if there is no consideration exchanged on both sides, then it's not a real contract.

The second C stands for Capacity. This means people cannot enter contracts with children or people suffering from mental disabilities. Both parties must have the "capacity" to enter the contract.

Lastly, the O is for an Object that is legal. You cannot enter a contract to murder someone. You cannot enter into a contract to bribe someone. The scheme, the materials contracted for, the activities envisioned, must all be possible and legal. Otherwise the contract is void under American law.

KINDS OF CONTRACTS

Just as the law constantly attempts to classify human conduct, it also endlessly classifies contracts and paperwork. In business, there are four main types of agreements: bilateral and unilateral contracts, implied agreements and quantum meruit claims.

BILATERAL CONTRACTS

These agreements are often called "a promise for a promise." Such a contract can be oral or written. The arrangement sets out, generally, what the parties are to do, approximately when, and for how much. Often, right after signing such a contract, nothing happens between the parties, for awhile. Behind the scenes, materials are being gathered, plans are made, extra employees are hired, and money is moved here and there. Because each side has made those promises, each party will rely on them, and begin investing money and time to get the contract completed. This whole system is the grease that runs the American economy.

UNILATERAL CONTRACTS

Unilateral contracts are a little different. They are a promise, in return for some act or work. Again, such a contract can be oral or written. They go something like this, "If you mow my lawn on Saturday, I will pay you $50.00." There is a promise of money, in return for an action. If there is no mowing on Saturday, there is no agreement. On the other hand, if the lawn has been cut, payment on the completed contract will be expected. If unpaid, upon proper evidence, the plaintiff lawn worker can sue the defendant homeowner for breach of the unilateral contract, and win.

IMPLIED AGREEMENTS

These contracts occur when some services or goods are supplied in a way that very strongly suggests that there is an expectation of payment. As you hurry to take a train in the morning you pass a newspaper stand, and a little dish with money in it sits nearby the stacks of papers. Commuters hurry past, pick up a paper, and drop some money in the dish. This is an implied contract, sometimes called implied-in-fact, because it is from the particular facts (the commuter gets a newspaper) that suggests there should be payment (there's a price, in money, right on the newspaper). Sitting down in a restaurant implies one will pay for any food consumed. Similarly, if you agree to buy a car and you begin driving it around with dealer plates on it, but haven't paid for it yet. The dealer will eventually sue and claim there was an implied contract of sale.

QUANTUM MERUIT

Quantum meruit is Latin for "the amount earned," and that's exactly what this contract theory is about. As in res ipsa loquitur accident cases, judges deciding contract cases would sometimes feel that, legally, a plaintiff who did some kind of work should win the case, but there was no real, enforceable contract in the traditional sense.

In these cases, the court would look to the amount of work that was done, and award the plaintiff a verdict on that basis. As the law developed, these became known as implied-in-law contracts, as the doctrine comes from the legal implication of the court's fundamental fairness, not the implied facts in the case.

This doctrine is the basis of a controversial rule that comes up every weekday night, in small claims cases, across America. Someone hires a mechanic to fix a squeak. The mechanic spends 10 hours and $1,000.00, but can't fix the noise. The car owner refuses to pay. The mechanic sues. Very often, the small claims court judge will award the mechanic a verdict, based on quantum meruit. So, remember, the contract must say: "The mechanic will be paid only if the squeak is fixed. If said squeak is not repaired completely, there will be no hourly, nor any materials charges." Otherwise, you will owe the mechanic money for their time, and for each part installed in your car.

NON DISCLOSURE AGREEMENTS

These contracts prevent one side, or both, from telling anyone about the secrets they learned in working with others. Originally, these were used to keep industrial and commercial formulas, methods and plans, confidential. Recently, these types of contracts have come under fire because they were used to cover up wrongdoing by executives and others. The trend in the law in this area is that such agreements cannot cover up crimes, and people who sign these agreements do not sign away any other rights they may have.

THE SON OF SAM LAW

Contracts concerning crimes are illegal. What about a book contract with a criminal who will write about crimes they committed?

New York State wrestled with this problem in the 1970's. People were concerned that serial murderer, David Berkowitz, might profit by writing a book about his crimes. The result was the Son of Sam Law. New York Executive Law Section 632a stated that any money a criminal received for their story went to the victims. In *Simon and Schuster, Inc. v. Members of New York State Crime Victims Board*, 502 U.S. 105 (1991), the U.S. Supreme Court ruled the law unconstitutional. Even a criminal has a First Amendment right to tell his or her story.

More recent trends provide notice to victims if a criminal is receiving money from a book. Then a conventional lawsuit can be brought by the victims to seize the profits. That was done in the case of O.J. Simpson, and his book,

"If I Did It." Sometimes, agreements about any future publications can be included in a defendant's plea bargaining agreement.

MINORS AND CAPACITY PROBLEMS

Minors are a special group under the law. They can breach a contract without consequences, unless the contract is for food, clothing or shelter. When one contracts with a minor, it is usually voidable, at the whim of the minor, or their parents. American law is full of cases involving magazine subscriptions, electronic games, contests, prizes and other deals that were all rendered invalid, by contracting with a minor. So too, people with diminished mental capacity cannot enter into valid contracts. In either case, any such contract needs to be with their legal guardian.

ADDITIONAL CLASSIFICATIONS

From the above, the reader can see how there are valid, void, voidable and unenforceable contracts. There are also executory (not fully performed) and executed (fully performed) contracts.

EQUITY

Finally, there is one last concept that the reader must be aware of. When all else in court fails, parties sometimes throw out this intellectual life preserver and ask for "equity." This doctrine requests the court to decide a case on basic fairness, or at least alerts the judge to the fact that there are other, mitigating circumstances, which are important, and should be considered.

Your author didn't have to rely on this too much during a long litigation career. But, there were a few cases...

12. WRITING CONTRACTS

Over the hundreds of years, as contract law developed, various concepts and theories emerged to make contracting, and the lawsuits that resulted, simpler and more efficient. As in all human endeavors, sometimes they succeeded, and sometimes they did not.

Writing contracts is a special skill. Lawyers, like most professionals, today, keep up with the times with mandatory continuing education. Contract law continues to evolve. The law on nondisclosure agreements has changed. Statutes of limitations have been modified in some jurisdictions. One of the most arcane areas is specifically what clauses and terms have been upheld recently. Law books contain reams of cases declaring this clause or that invalid. Some contracts must be written with certain words and a certain size type. During litigation, contracts and leases are often found to be full of old clauses that have since been declared void, changed in meaning or "unenforceable because they are against modern public policy."

People in business do not need the skills of a great contract writer. All that is needed is the basics, so that the daily, commercial grind of work can be safely navigated. In the background, good managers are always on the lookout for any big problems with contracts, contractors or suppliers. Contractual issues that cause big problems for a company will require hiring a good business lawyer.

DOES IT HAVE TO BE IN WRITING?

There's a common misunderstanding that a written contract is more valid, more enforceable, than an oral one. This may stem from the fact that, in a case involving a written contract, a lot more money can be involved, and it is usually easier to prove the terms that were agreed to. However, to the courts, both contracts, once they are proved to exist, are equal.

If there is a dispute, an oral contract can be proved, or refuted, by the testimony of the parties. Witnesses can be called if they overheard the plaintiff and defendant talking about their arrangement. Relevant testimony may establish what the parties did, after the alleged agreement, to show whether they acted as if there was a contract or not. Notes on scraps of paper, business records, diagrams, memos, blueprints, models, plans, bank accounts, audio and video tapes, phone messages, and other physical items can also be used to prove that an oral agreement existed.

Of course, a written contract is right there, printed, for everyone to see. However, different types of writing can be assembled and become a contract. A series of letters, or emails, can form a written contract. Texts, back and forth, company memos, correspondence, all have been held to constitute, as a whole, a written contract.

THE STATUTE OF FRAUDS

Going back hundreds of years, swindlers, and grifters periodically caused legal problem by skillfully lying about oral agreements they allegedly made. Sometimes the oral agreement gave them title to land, from a rich relative, now deceased. Or they were hired by a former manager of a business, to do a lot of work, but were never paid. In this way, shady claimants would try to score. Finally, in the late 1600's, the English government got around to creating a law specifically naming which contracts had to be in writing. This law still exists today. It is called the Statute of Frauds because its purpose is to prevent fraud.

New York has a Statute of Frauds. So does California. But, so typical of our quirky system, you will not find the actual words "Statute of Frauds" in the laws themselves. New York's is hidden in its General Obligations Law. GOB § 5-701, is its Statute of Frauds. And one requirement, that contracts over $500.00 be in writing, is not in the GOL. It's in another law, New York's Uniform Commercial Code, § 2-201, which does mention the Statute of Frauds. In California, you will find the statute in Civil Code § 1624.

The actual written laws, and the resulting case law around them, have many a twist and turn in the minute details. If you can remember the word, F.R.A.U.D., you can remember the major contracts which must be in writing in most states.

F stands for Five hundred dollars. If the contract is for more than five hundred bucks, it needs to be in writing.

R is for Real estate. If the contract involves the purchase of land, then the amount does not matter, the contract has to be in writing. There is one important exception. If someone "orally" sells land to another, the contract is normally void. But, if the buyer can prove they made payments and then actually began making improvements, they can ask a court for "specific performance" of the contract. This will prevent the "unjust enrichment" of the crooked seller, who wants to take back the improved property. Also, some short room rentals can be oral.

A is for Annual contracts. If the contract will definitely take longer than a year to perform, then it must be written. Managers must be careful of oral arrangements that might turn into a long-term situation for their company. Any oral contract based on how long someone will live can be valid, because it may not take more than a year. For example, take this sentence: "The company won't evict you, Mrs. Jones, as long as you live there." That is a valid oral contract because Mrs. Jones may die tomorrow. Other oral arrangements, that extend employment, or some other arrangement, beyond the one year time limit, will need to be written out and signed.

U is for United in marriage. This is a relic of the past that has had a resurgence in prenuptial and postnuptial agreements. If a promise is made by one mate to the other, contingent on marriage, it has to be in writing and signed. That means that agreements as to what someone will give to the other, after the marriage, or how much people can weigh during the marriage (don't laugh), cannot be oral.

D is for the Debt of another. In the United States you are never supposed to be forced to pay for other's debts. To do so is usually very odd, indeed. Whenever a person agrees to pay a debt for another (i.e., co-signing for a loan) that agreement must be in writing.

The workings of the statute came to light in a 2019 case involving President Donald Trump's former lawyer, Michael Cohen. He was in jail for campaign finance violations, fraud and lying to Congress. But he was still racking up huge legal bills while being further investigated by New York's Attorney General. Cohen sued Trump, on an alleged 2017 contract with him, to get him to pay his legal bills. Cohen claimed he had an oral assurance that his legal bills would continue to be paid. The judge said that the law does not allow an oral agreement to be extended forever. Brown, Stephen R. "Cohen Hits Snag." *N.Y. Daily News*, 30 Aug., 2019.

IS THE WRITING ADEQUATE?

Well, now we know what categories of contracts must be in writing to be enforced. But, how do we judge the actual papers we are looking at? What do we look for to determine if what we are holding in our hands is a valid contract or not?

The first thing any valid contract must contain are what are known as the essential terms of the agreement. Can you tell what was agreed to by each party? Surprisingly, major items, like the price of things that are bought and sold all the time, or the date of delivery, can sometimes be left out, and the contract will still be enforceable. The court will simply substitute "a reasonable price" and "a reasonable date of delivery," if there's litigation over the document.

If necessary, and for many different reasons, written contracts can refer to other documents, and "incorporate them by reference" into the agreement. So lists of goods, maps, blueprints and schedules are often attached to written contracts and become part of them.

Another thing is the signature. It can be electronic, or a stamp. If a person is illiterate, they can mark an "x" as their signature or use a carved wooden block for that purpose. Usually the signature should appear at the end. Corrections and changes should be initialed by each party, in the margin, of the contract.

ELECTRONIC SIGNATURES

When you go online, and you buy something, you put in your bank code, and the expiration date of your credit card, and what state you live in. All those little things you are doing are electronically signing the order form for you. Those answers will be used, in court, if necessary, to identify you and prove that it could only have been you that entered the sales contract to buy those goods online. These procedures are covered in the Electronic Signature in Global and National Commerce Act, 15 U.S.C. § 96.

Under some circumstances, both parties do not need to sign the document. Only the party to be charged (the one sued) must have signed the agreement. Therefore, one must be wary of people who get you to sign a contract but refuse to sign it themselves. Usually, that's an attempt to be able to enforce the contract against you but prevent you from doing the same thing. An argument over just such a signature came up in Stormy Daniels' 2018 California case against President Trump. The porn star sued Trump, claiming he did not sign the nondisclosure agreement that prevented her from telling her story of their alleged year-long 2006 love affair. Her case was eventually dismissed. Sommerfeldt, Chris. "Donald Exposed." *N.Y. Daily News*, 7 Mar., 2018, p. 11.

ONCE THINGS HIT THE FAN

Let's say the legal department did the best they could. The executives of the company did their best. Nevertheless, litigation over a contract has begun. Now, certain other concepts come into play.

THE PECULIARITIES OF CONTRACT LAW INTERPRETATION

Contract law has a long history. Many rules and guidelines have been developed to aid jurists in interpreting contracts. The Internet is full of scholarly papers on the subject. We will only scratch the surface here, in a very general way.

First is the idea that ordinary words in contracts are given their usual meanings, but technical words are given the technical meaning in the particular industry they are used in. So, if the contract is simple, about shoes, and dollars, most courts can decide it. But if a company is selling atomic proton thingamajigs, then the parties had better be ready to explain to the judge, and jury, just what they are. Often, that takes some kind of costly expert testimony.

If there is a mistake in a contract, it goes against whoever wrote that part of the document. Often, during negotiations with multiple parties, one side or the other takes the lead, and has their attorneys draft, and print out, all the final documents for execution. The final contract may be in a jacket, or blueback, that has the law firm's name on it. If there is any litigation over that contract, the lawsuit will reveal any mistake, or ambiguity, in those papers. If so, the interpretation of that portion of the contract will go against whichever party hired the lawyers who wrote the contract.

Another well-known adage is that specific contract terms are more important than general ones. So, if a company makes cars, all their contracts should state the specific make, and model each agreement applies to, rather than just using the word "cars."

There is also a set of rules that establish the "pecking order" of the words on the page itself. Not all writing is created equal. Any words in the contract that are in a preprinted form (i.e., printed by a printing press) are the lowest on the totem pole. They are part of the contract, as long as they are not crossed out, or superseded by other writing in the document. In the electronic age, this is becoming rarer, but any typewritten words override the printed ones. The king of all words, in a contract, are any handwritten notations, made in pen and initialed by the parties. They take precedence over anything else in the document.

THE PAROL EVIDENCE RULE

Oral evidence is sometimes called parol evidence, a term derived from French. Basically, the rule forbids oral evidence, and some other types of proof, to modify the terms of a contract once it is signed. There are some exceptions to the rule. Oral evidence is usually okay to show fraud, or that a mistake, or a typographical error, was made in a contract. But, generally, in business, a written contract will stand on its own, and can be difficult to get out of.

We have now seen that some contracts must be in writing and have to be "signed" somehow. Contracts can incorporate other documents in them, and written ones usually cannot be changed without a new, signed document.

Now, what happens when a contract is breached?

13. REMEDIES FOR BREACH OF CONTRACT

Contract drafters do their best to create good, clear agreements. Nevertheless, companies fail, people don't live up to their obligations and unforeseen things occur. So, breaches of contracts happen all the time in America. What remedies does one have, in that case?

WHAT IS A BREACH?

A breach of a contract occurs whenever one side does not fulfill its obvious duties under the agreement.

A lot of legal arguing goes on about whether someone's performance under a contract has been completed, has been substantially completed, or is just plain inferior. Some legal wrangling also goes into the issue of whether a breach is minor or material. The smart manager understands that a bad contractual situation can sometimes be salvaged by a last-ditch effort at conforming to the contractual terms. Trying to work things out, and remaining calm and reasonable, can go a long way in convincing a jury of your position, in a later trial.

THE TENDER OFFER IN CONTRACT DISPUTES

There are many examples of tendering, in American law. You can tender your resignation. You can run a tender business (look it up). In the contractual context, it means offering to perform a contract.

If an argument has started over some agreement, a written message that you (or your company) are tendering (offering) your performance, can sometimes save you. Tendering your contractual performance is like throwing down the gauntlet. You are basically saying that, on the date of the message, you were ready, willing and able to go ahead with the work. If the other person now breaks off contact, continues to argue, refuses to work, or refuses to pay, you may have saved your bacon. In some cases, if you properly "tender your performance," in a timely manner, you cannot be the party who breached the contract.

Don't get me wrong. There will still be a big fight over it in court. Was there a tender? Was the message sent? Was it too late? But you'll probably win.

MONEY DAMAGES

The first type of relief an entity can get for a breach of contract is hard, cold cash. The most basic of money damages are called compensatory damages, because they "compensate" the plaintiff for the loss suffered. In truth, when a party gets compensatory damages, especially in contract cases, they usually lose a lot of money. That's because, out of that payment (if it's ever collected) will usually come attorney's fees, and all court costs, exhibits and witness' expenses.

The math of compensatory damages works like this. John and Mary enter a bilateral contract (a promise for a promise) concerning books. John promises to pay $10.00 for 10 business law books, for a total of $100.00. Martha promises to deliver the books in one week. When the date for the delivery comes up, Martha tells John she cannot get the books, after all. This is a material breach. John now must buy the 10 books from bookseller number 2, Joan, who charges him $20.00, each. That's a total of $200.00. Since the books cost him more money, John can sue Martha for $100.00 compensatory damages for her breach of the contract.

CONSEQUENTIAL DAMAGES

Not all contracts are equally important to a business. Sometimes, companies have contracts with multiple suppliers and can pick and choose who they want to do business with. But some contracts can be crucial for a company. Both sides of a contract sometimes know that, if one side breaches, the other party will lose substantial business income as a result. For instance, a manufacturer's business stops without raw materials. Any number of tech companies stop doing business if the flow of data stops. So, a second type of money damages exists, called consequential damages. These are losses that happen as a "consequence" of the breach of contract. These claims are seen in cases where contractual work was not performed on a commercial vehicle, delaying its return to service. The breach of contract caused the truck owner to lose profits, which can be claimed as consequential damages.

LIQUIDATED DAMAGES

What a crazy name for a legal term. It has nothing to do with water. In business, liquidating means the entire process of converting an asset to cash, usually by figuring out how much something is really worth and then selling it. In terms of damages, liquidated means that the damages of a breach of contract have already been figured out (i.e., they have been liquidated) and both sides agree to those numbers.

But life is never that simple. Your narrator had a case in which our office represented a client who owned a restaurant. He felt bullied for years by his linen supply company. They didn't work like other firms. A guy from the linen company would come to the restaurant, once every two weeks. He would take over the place. He didn't listen to anybody. Every table got completely changed, regardless if it was already pristine. He ordered all new napkins and tablecloths, which the restaurant owner felt was not necessary. My client finally threw him out, stopped paying and got a new supplier that listened to him. He got sued immediately.

Our law firm was shocked when the plaintiff's lawyer claimed our client had already agreed to a very high liquidated damages amount! Luckily, the liquidated damages formula was on the back of a faded sales receipt, and whether the client actually ever saw it, or signed it, was questionable. The case settled for peanuts.

NOMINAL DAMAGES

Always remember that a jury can award you $1.00 if it does not like you. That's called 'nominal" (very small) damages.

What a jury might not know is that there are cases on record where the "winner" of the measly dollar didn't give up. They appealed. They got the

$1.00 thrown out, as a mistake by the jury. So, the case had to be re-tried, solely on the issue of damages, and the plaintiff ended up making a lot of money.

MITIGATION

Mitigation is a legal concept that always softens some injury or punishment. In contract law, a plaintiff must mitigate (lessen) the damages from a breach of contract that she or he can. For example, assume a company contracts to move goods with a trucker. The company moves its products outside, on the agreed date, to load onto the expected delivery truck. The defendant truck owner, however, then clearly breaches the contract by not showing up with the vehicle. The plaintiff company has a duty to prevent its goods from getting damaged, while outside. So too, if a person is fired in breach of their employment contract, there is a duty to mitigate, by trying to find another job.

RESCISSION

This remedy basically "rescinds" the entire agreement, as if it never existed. Everything exchanged gets returned, and everybody moves on with their lives.

RESTITUTION

Making restitution, with regard to contracts, is returning part, or all, of the consideration that formed the basis of the contract agreement. It is usually money, but it can be in the form of goods or materials. This is often done, hand in hand, with rescission, to properly balance what is owed to each party.

SPECIFIC PERFORMANCE

This is an equitable contract remedy, meaning it is used to prevent unjust enrichment of one side of a contract, at the expense of the other. It is used in real estate contract cases, and agreements about buying rare art or antiques. Because these items are unique, plaintiffs will sometimes still want the contract of sale to go through, although there was some breach of contract by the seller. Specific performance is the remedy. It asks the court to force the defendant to specifically go ahead and perform the contract.

Specific performance is not permitted for personal services contracts. For instance, if a barber was forced to specifically perform a haircut contract, he or she might quickly shave the plaintiff's head, in spite, instead.

REFORMATION

This remedy "reforms" any mistakes in the contract, so that the agreement properly reflects the parties' intentions. However, the court determines those intentions, and the parties may not agree with the judge's decision.

ENFORCING REMEDIES

The court has various means of enforcing judgments and collecting money for breaches of contract or any other purpose under law. It can "attach" (seize) property of a litigant and sell it. The court can also "garnish" (take part of) any bank accounts or wages owed to the defendant.

INJUNCTIVE RELIEF

An injunction is an order by a court to refrain from doing something. You hear of them, often, during strikes. The company will seek an injunction stopping the strike, while the union may seek an injunction against the company's union busting activities.

14. NEGOTIABLE INSTRUMENTS

Negotiable instruments are contracts that have a certain form. Because of this specific format, the documents themselves can be traded, and exchanged, for money, goods and services, and used as collateral. These contracts can represent huge amounts of money, but they are far easier and safer than carrying heavy suitcases full of cash. The importance of the entire negotiable instruments system in America, and the world, cannot be overstated. Since many of these instruments inject credit into the economy, they are the grease that keeps our economic wheels spinning smoothly. Even with the digital revolution, our negotiable instruments system will be around for many decades to come. Many of the rules that govern the negotiable instruments of today will eventually evolve and apply to the electronic versions of tomorrow.

Businesses need at least a rudimentary understanding of this world, as they will come in contact with it on a daily basis.

IN A CERTAIN FORM?

To explain this, we have to go back to the early 1940's. Various bar associations and legal organizations in the United States were distressed at the patchwork of commercial laws across America. They felt a more uniform set of business regulations were needed so that growing companies could expand, and ship goods, across state borders without legal difficulty. This was becoming especially important with World War II going on.

A couple of the major associations got together and created the Uniform Commercial Code. All the states and Washington D.C. have adopted at least parts of this Code. Article 3 concerns itself specifically with negotiable instruments. It sets out what negotiable contracts have to say, how they have to look, and how they need to be signed. Much of what follows comes from this statute. Almost all these contracts must be unconditional, meaning that, once it is signed, the document can be exchanged for money or goods just by being presented. No other conditions need to be met.

DRAFTS AND CHECKS

A draft is a document that tells someone who is holding money for someone else, to pay that money to a third person. Here is an example: If A owes B $500 and B owes C $500, B can write a draft instructing A to pay C. Then he gives that document to C. If the paper clearly has the instructions, the amount, the parties' names, and the date, it is a valid negotiable draft. A can be sued if the money is not transferred to C, as requested.

A check is one of the forms a draft can take. It is called a "check" because it always has a bank as the one doing the paying. Other than that, it's a draft, like any other.

Because drafts always have a draft writer, a money holder, and a draft receiver, they are called "three-party instruments," although they are usually only signed by one person.

NOTES

A note, or promissory note, is a two-party negotiable instrument, although, again, it is usually signed by only one individual. These documents record loans, from one person, or firm, to another. Banks, finance companies and wealthy individuals all lend money through this system. When you view one of these documents, it will always say who borrowed the money, and who lent it, how much, when it was lent, and it will state that the borrower promises to pay the money back, with interest. It is executed, or signed, by the person borrowing the money.

These notes can be "secured." That means they are "backed up," by giving the lender a lien on something valuable. If the note is backed up by a lien on a house, or land, it's called a mortgage. If it's backed up by a lien on a car, it's called a car loan.

CD'S

A certificate of deposit is also a negotiable instrument. It is a special note, sort of a reverse promissory note. A bank, or some other financial institution, is the borrower. In return for the use of the cash, the bank promises to pay the money back at a later time, with interest. This is not a bank account. One cannot deposit more money nor take money out of a traditional certificate. Because these are negotiable, they can be traded and used to secure other loans and deals.

SIGNING DOCUMENTS AND AGENCY

During a long business career, employees and independent contractors are sometimes called upon to sign documents for others. Usually, it's routine mail or paychecks. But, once in awhile, they may be called upon to execute a document that involves a breathtaking amount of money, for their corporation, or boss.

Normally, a person signing on behalf of another is acting as an agent. The person who they sign for is called the principal. This is an agency relationship. The agent is the servant. The principal is the boss and is responsible for any contracts the agent enters. However, there are rare times when an agent can sign a document for a principal and expose themselves to millions of dollars of potential liability.

For example, in a contract, when a person signs their boss' name first, and then writes "By:_____" and signs with their own name, they are making clear that they are acting as the agent of the other person. This binds their boss into the contract, and normally releases the agent from any personal liability. Any attorney would know to sue the boss, not the agent, for any breach of contract.

However, if that agency is not revealed, and the worker simply signs their own name, they can be held personally responsible, if there is a breach of contract. Certainly, if the agency is discovered, any plaintiff in that situation will sue both, the agent, and the principal, for the breach. But the above fact pattern is a telling reminder to always watch carefully when others want you to sign something for them.

15. HOW TO ORGANIZE YOUR BUSINESS

So many people today are starting their own businesses, some thought was given to providing a brief section to serve as a reminder of what is possible, and some of the pros and cons of each. After you have created your business plan, and have your budget ready, consider these options.

THE SOLE PROPRIETORSHIP

This is the simplest way to organize a business. At most, you just file a certificate of doing business, if you want to operate under a business name.

The good thing about this kind of organization is control. You can move fast if need be. You control everything. And that is also the bad side. You have to open the bank accounts. You rent the premises, buy the delivery van, etc. You must put all the money in, to start the business, and, at first, you are the only employee. As you grow, your responsibilities will increase, until you need help. As you get bigger, incorporating may become a good idea. If the business fails, you will usually lose everything.

THE PARTNERSHIP

This has some advantages over the sole proprietorship. In this arrangement, usually, the expenses, and the work to be done, are divided among the partners. It results in a more efficient, powerful organization. The partners concentrate on what they are good at. Often people with skills that complement each other can make a formidable money-making team.

On the downside, you will need a partnership contract. It may require the services of an attorney, depending on how complex the business will be. You are not independent in this kind of business arrangement. Trust and honesty are crucial. Each partner needs to be kept in the loop. And when things go south, a partnership is very much like a bad marriage. You are stuck. The courts, in your author's experience, don't help much. They quickly dissolve the partnership and tell the former associates to go divvy up the assets. If the parties cannot agree, the court divides it up. There will usually be a winner and a loser. The business rarely survives. That's it.

THE CORPORATION

Whether it's a professional corporation or a regular business structure, this is the way to go for big organizations. These companies can grow into global behemoths. Usually, an attorney creates the corporation for you. This type of business has a uniform structure, allowing information to filter up to the top, and changes and improvements (supposedly) to come down to the street. Everyone has a title, a role and a salary.

On the bad side, everyone can lose their shirt. Lousy leaders can end up on top hiring incompetent family members. Corporate voting, and all the little formalities of meetings, minutes, and corporate resolutions can be cumbersome, expensive and a pain in the neck when the company starts to grow. Profits can be promised to so many people there is no money left for the company itself. Savings plans, tax consequences, dividends and the SEC make this the most complex option.

HOW DO YOU FIND THAT GOOD BUSINESS ATTORNEY?

At various times in this volume, the author has suggested that it is important to know when to call a good attorney. But how do you find one?

Like any other important process, this takes an investment in time, and maybe a little money. Clients are sometimes surprised by how small the legal community is. In special areas of the law, a medium sized city may only have two or three lawyers that handle a certain type of case. And they all know each other. Therefore, in all initial consultation contacts with attorneys, one must discuss a possible conflict of interest, first. Make sure the lawyer you talk to has no association with the party you are in a dispute with. It's rare, but it happens.

The first suggestion that should always be made in a search for a lawyer is the local bar association. Almost all local (by county) bar associations have programs to help find the right lawyer. The associations categorize their members into lists of specialties. A person can call and get a name of someone who is a real estate attorney, or who specializes in criminal defense. Usually, these first one-hour bar referral appointments, are free. The investment comes in vetting these people. You must put in the time to go see them, research them, ask around. You want to see how you feel about this person representing you, or your company, in front of a judge or a board of directors. Note their experience, presentation, assistants and use of technology. If the first firm isn't satisfactory, it is very important not to be discouraged. One can get another recommendation and see someone else.

Another route to finding a lawyer is searching the media. If you need a good lawyer in a certain discipline, then do searches with Google, and whatever else you have at your disposal, for prior similar cases that were reported in the news. Then get in touch with that successful law firm.

Of course, there is law firm advertising. Many big law firms advertise in trade publications or newspapers. Industry associations may also have connections to knowledgeable attorneys in particular fields. And, of course, there's always good old word of mouth. Discreetly inquiring of colleagues, or friends, if they know of a good lawyer can also yield good results.

16. COMMON LEGAL MISCONCEPTIONS

People sometimes have certain ideas about the law that your narrator has found to be wrong, or misconstrued, in some way. Here are some of the more common ones that are heard today.

"If the president dies, the vice president must be sworn in right away!" Wrong. No swearing in is needed. When the president's heart stops, the vice president becomes the president. Automatically.

"Owning a corporation protects you from personal liability." Totally wrong. A corporation usually only protects you from corporate debts. Banks and people in business know this. So, if you own a new, small corporation, you will be required to personally sign for loans and services, or else you won't get them. So, there's no protection from personal liability there, after all, especially when you first start out.

"After I die, no one will fight over my stuff." People do the best they can with estate planning. But, if someone leaves a lot of money, people will fight over it.

"Seven years is a legal time limit that applies to a lot of legal situations." Just the opposite. Statutes of limitations range from 90 days to six years. A judgment is good for 10 years. "Seven years" hardly ever appears in the law. 'Don't know where that started.

"Common law marriages are very common." No. They are very rare, today. Most states, like New York, abolished them. Alabama and Colorado still have them. Other states only recognize unions before a certain date, or only for inheritance purposes. It is true, though, that, if you are in a valid common law marriage, you need a real, formal divorce to get out of it.

"A person can act as an attorney and a witness at the same time." Once in awhile, on TV, you may see a comedic character question himself, by switching roles. That's not permitted in real life. The roles are thought to be incompatible by the courts.

"The judges on television are really good." In real courtrooms around the nation, hard working judges strive mightily to maintain the decorum of their rooms on a daily basis. They usually deal with people with respect. Attorneys themselves are no shrinking violets. Experienced lawyers have been around and know a lousy judge when they see one. And their friends are often highly placed judges and politicians. They will not be talked to the way TV judges address litigants. Lawyers know what committees to complain to. On TV, there's no appeal if your judge acts like a clown.

"Hollywood is really accurate when it depicts court room scenes." This statement is truly laughable. Often, these productions have technical advisers. One can only assume they simply disregard them, and exercise poetic license. Most scenes in court are overly dramatic, childish and silly. The most authentic movie your author ever saw about his specialty, litigation, was "The Verdict" with Paul Newman.

"All lawyers make a lot of money." 'Simply not true. Many attorneys must supplement their income by writing books!

17. YOUR LIFE PLAN

This writer has had many an inquiry from people about what they need in life, legally, as they move forward. There are ethical considerations about dispensing direct legal advice in certain settings, so I always felt my statements on this subject would need to be very general. Some of these things are difficult, but necessary, to contemplate. Anyway, this is what I say.

Most people need four legal documents in their life. They are a health care proxy, a will, a living will, and a power of attorney.

THE HEALTH CARE PROXY

A health care proxy appoints someone you trust with your life to make decisions for you if you are unconscious. That's it. You can place some limits on the authority you extend.

THE WILL

Of course, a will gives away the property of the decedent, legally called the testator. The more property an individual has, the more planning they will need to do, to dispose of the property exactly the way they want. The surrogate court (a/k/a/probate court) is in charge of dividing up the estates of the deceased. After a person passes, the will is filed with the court, and probate begins.

Because a will must be proved in the surrogate's court, there are always some expenses involved. So, the trend today is to avoid probate, completely, with "transfer on death" (TOD) designations and beneficiaries on trust accounts. That way the property passes without going through probate at all.

To use this method, one must be very careful that each piece of property has been properly registered for the beneficiary desired. If the estate is very large, estate taxes can still become an issue and professional legal advice is called for.

One mistake to avoid is in one's burial instructions. They are often contained in the will. Unfortunately, in many cases, the will cannot be located, for a week or so, after the testator's death. Lawyers lounges always have a few stories about the client who was cremated and had their ashes spread over the ocean. Then the lawyer found the missing will, which specified a burial at a local cemetery, where a plot was already purchased.

Make your wishes known to your loved ones, if any, before you leave. Perhaps write a letter or two about the subject and leave copies in obvious places. And make sure your will is not locked in a safe deposit box that will take weeks, and a court order, to open. Leave a copy in a top drawer somewhere and one with your lawyer. You can even file it in court before you die.

LIVING WILL

The name of this document is confusing. The name presumably comes from the fact that a person's testamentary will only comes into effect after death. This document is signed while you are still alive (living) and it tells your doctors what to do when you are near death (your will). Hence, "living will." It is also sometimes referred to as a "directive to physicians," which is a more logical title.

The living will is different than then a health care proxy. It does not involve a third person. It directs your doctors to stop treatment that prolongs your life when there is no hope of recovery.

POWER OF ATTORNEY

This is another document that you should have ready in case the worst happens and you are incapacitated. Again, you need to choose a person, or persons, that you implicitly trust, as it gives another human being a lot of control over your legal affairs.

In this document, you name the person that you are giving power of attorney to. They do not need to be a lawyer. The name is derived from the idea that you are giving another person the powers that a lawyer possesses when they represent others.

In the document you clearly indicate what legal actions the person may take on your behalf. Some common ones are paying rent, paying mortgage payments, performing banking transactions, paying taxes, and paying insurance premiums.

HAVE A FINANCIAL PLAN

If there is anything important to impart to people, it is the need for some kind of investment plan for the future. Too many Americans find themselves impoverished in their old age for no reason other than a lack of education in economics. Your plan need not be the best. Just create one and try to stick to it.

One of the great things about Wall Street is that, on what is called the "retail" level, it does not discriminate. If you buy shares in a company, or a mutual fund, nobody cares what your name is, or where you live or what troubles you have had in the past. They will send you the dividends and interest payments. You don't have to be the same religion or come from the same country. The clerks doing the work do not know who you are, and don't care. It can be difficult to hold onto investments for long periods, through emergencies and raising children, but that's the key to success.

BE CLEVER

Observation is crucial. Watch for ways to gather capital and improve your life. In the 17th century, astronomers in Europe figured out the distance to the sun, and then the speed of light, by combining the smallest scraps of data, to reach the correct conclusions. The numbers were so enormous that many scientists did not believe them. They were not proven correct for almost a century. So, especially, watch for small things that are harbingers of big things to come.

'BEST OF LUCK

Not many subjects are such a large part of your life as the law. Time spent studying it always yields its own rewards.

Good luck!

TABLE OF AUTHORITIES

Cases

Statutes

Other Authorities

INDEX

ABOUT THE AUTHOR

James F. Cirrincione is an attorney from Yonkers, New York. He attended Pace University, and New York Law School. He began working as a lawyer in 1978, for the Employers Insurance Company of Wausau, in its Manhattan office. He spent 15 years in the insurance industry, defending all types of property damage and personal injury claims in depositions, arbitrations and jury trials around the New York metropolitan area. From 1993 to 2010 he was in private practice, in the Bronx, specializing in construction accidents and malpractice cases. The author began his writing career in 1983, for a company newsletter. By 1989 he was writing professionally for several publications. His articles appeared in The New York Times, The Atlantic Flyer pilot's newspaper, and the Northeast Weekend Flyers magazine. In 1994 his book, "Taking Depositions," was published by LRP Publications, in Pennsylvania. As of this writing, Mr. Cirrincione teaches law at a local college, and acts as a consultant on litigation issues.

Made in the USA
Middletown, DE
13 September 2020

18729133R00104